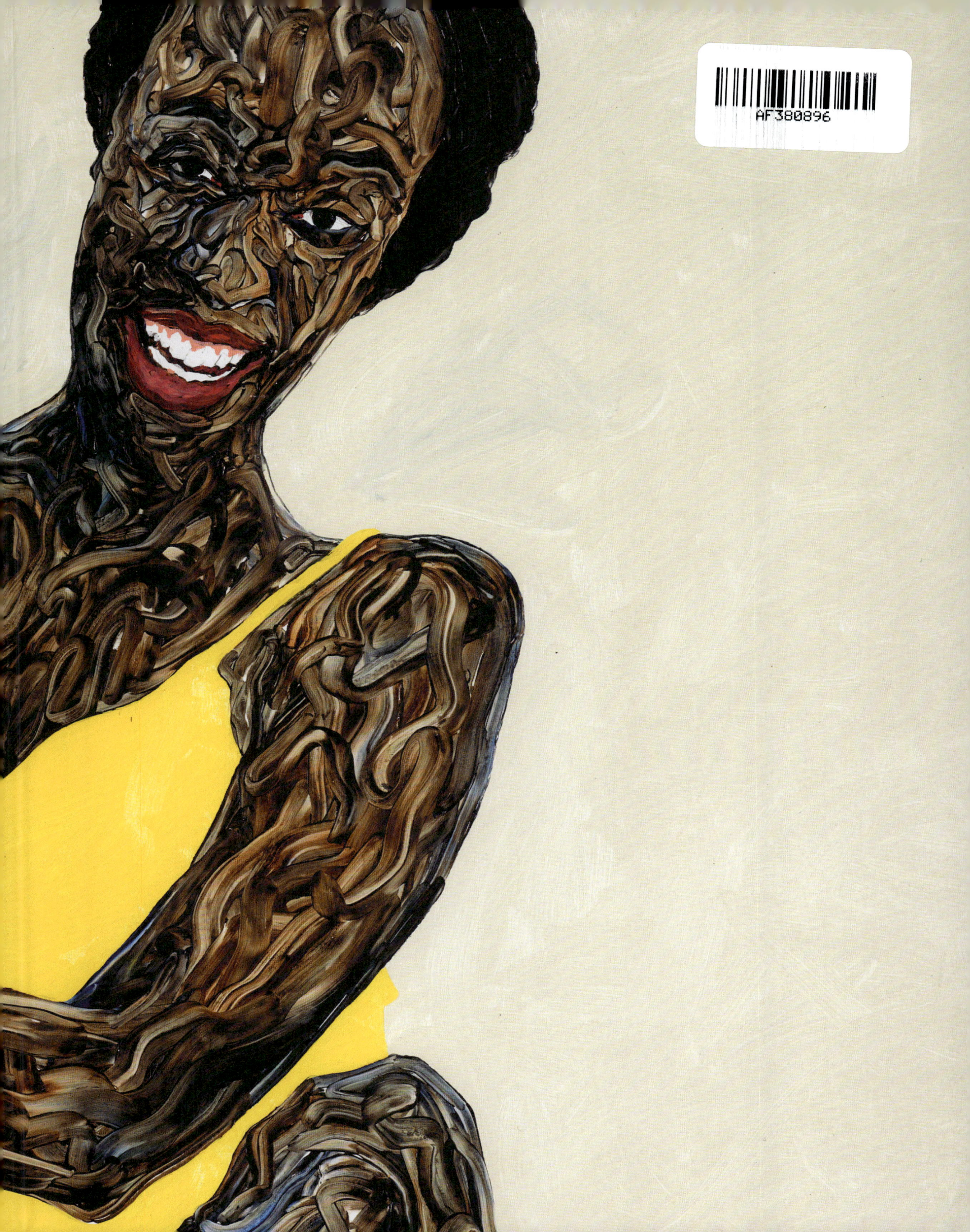

AF380896

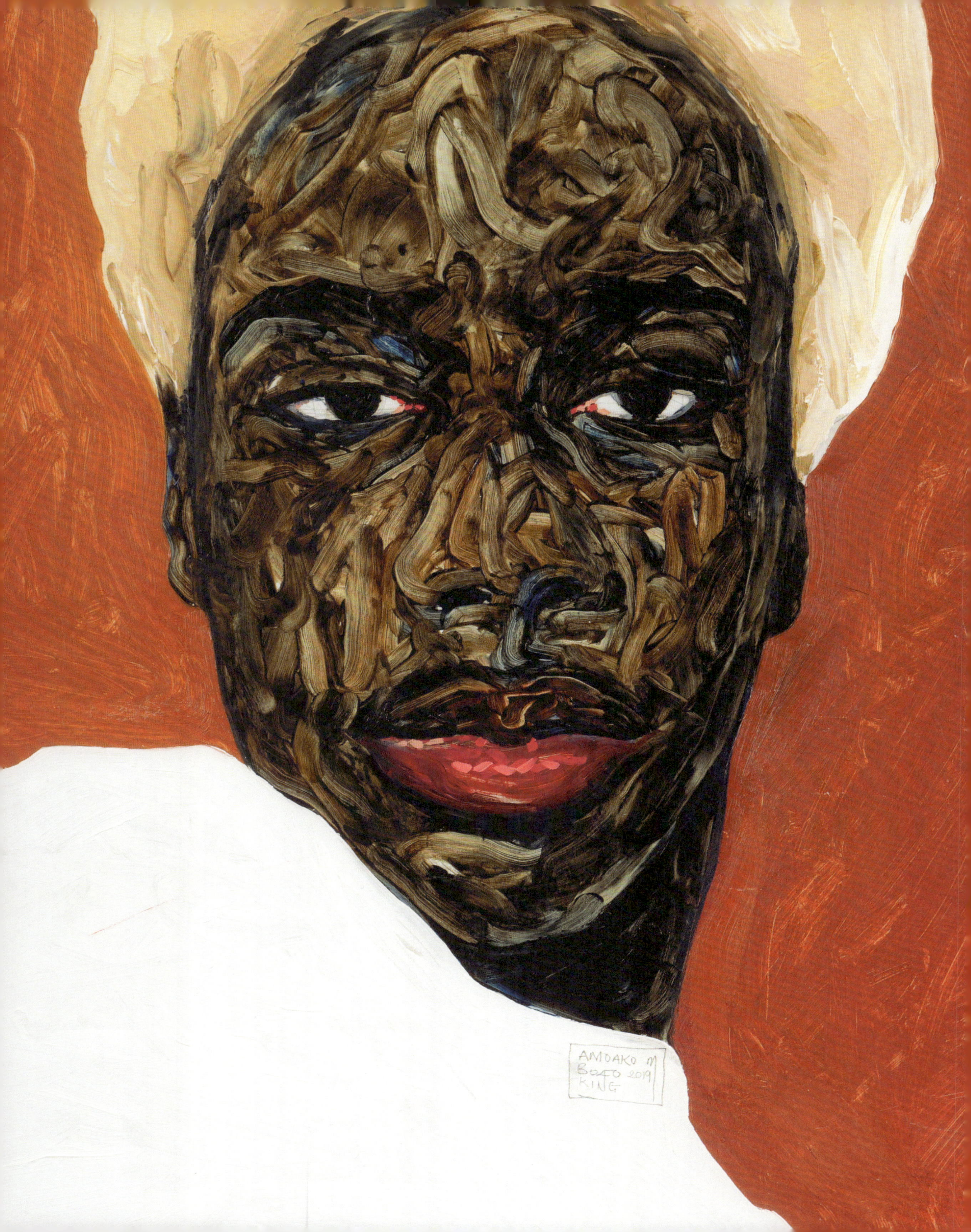

AMOAKO M
BOAFO 2019
KING

Amoako Boafo
Proper Love

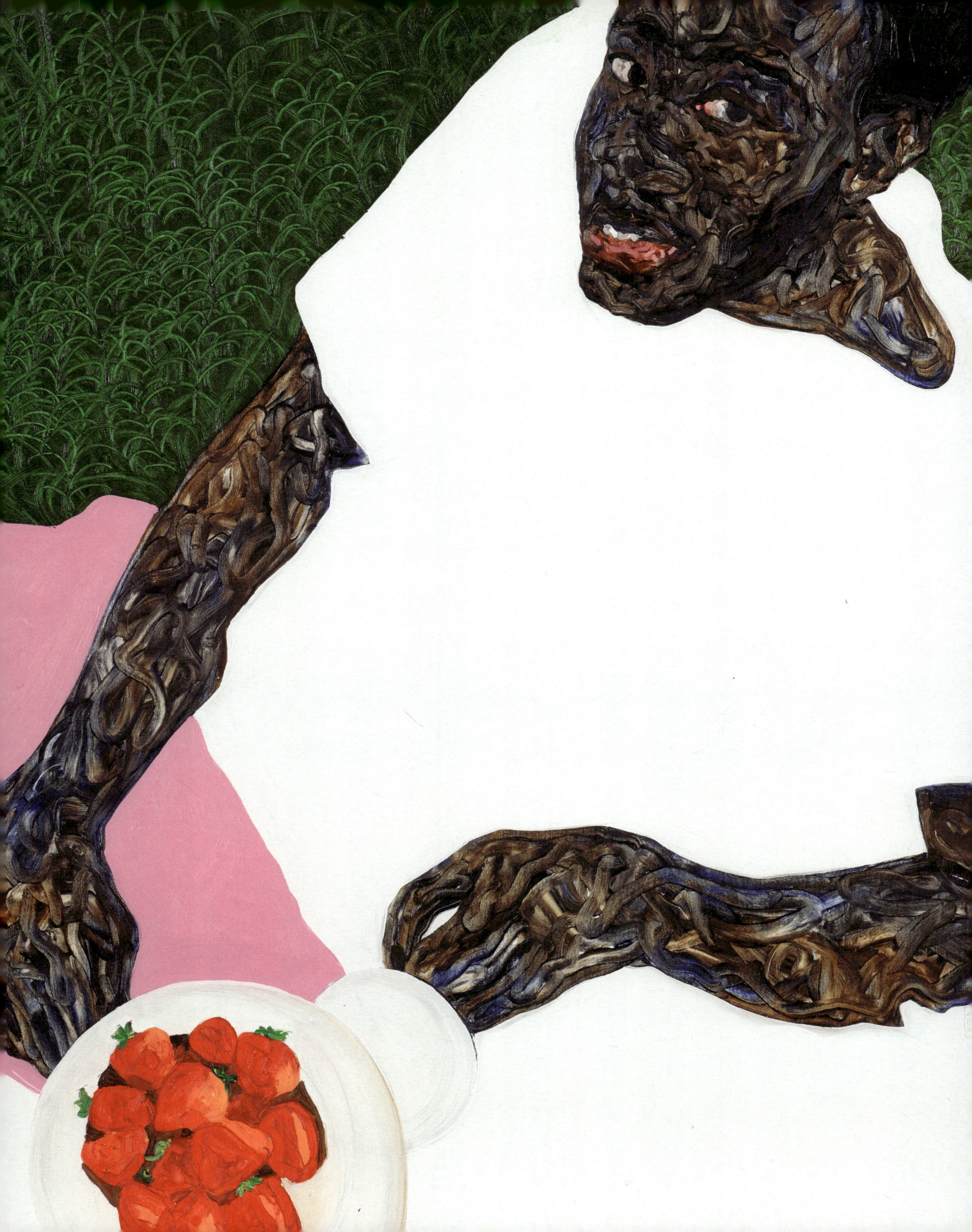

Amoako Boafo

Proper Love

Edited by Stella Rollig and Sergey Harutoonian

With contributions by Amoako Boafo, Ekow Eshun, Sergey Harutoonian, Mahret Ifeoma Kupka, Stella Rollig, Taiye Selasi, and Vasilena Stoyanova

Verlag der Buchhandlung
Walther und Franz König, Cologne

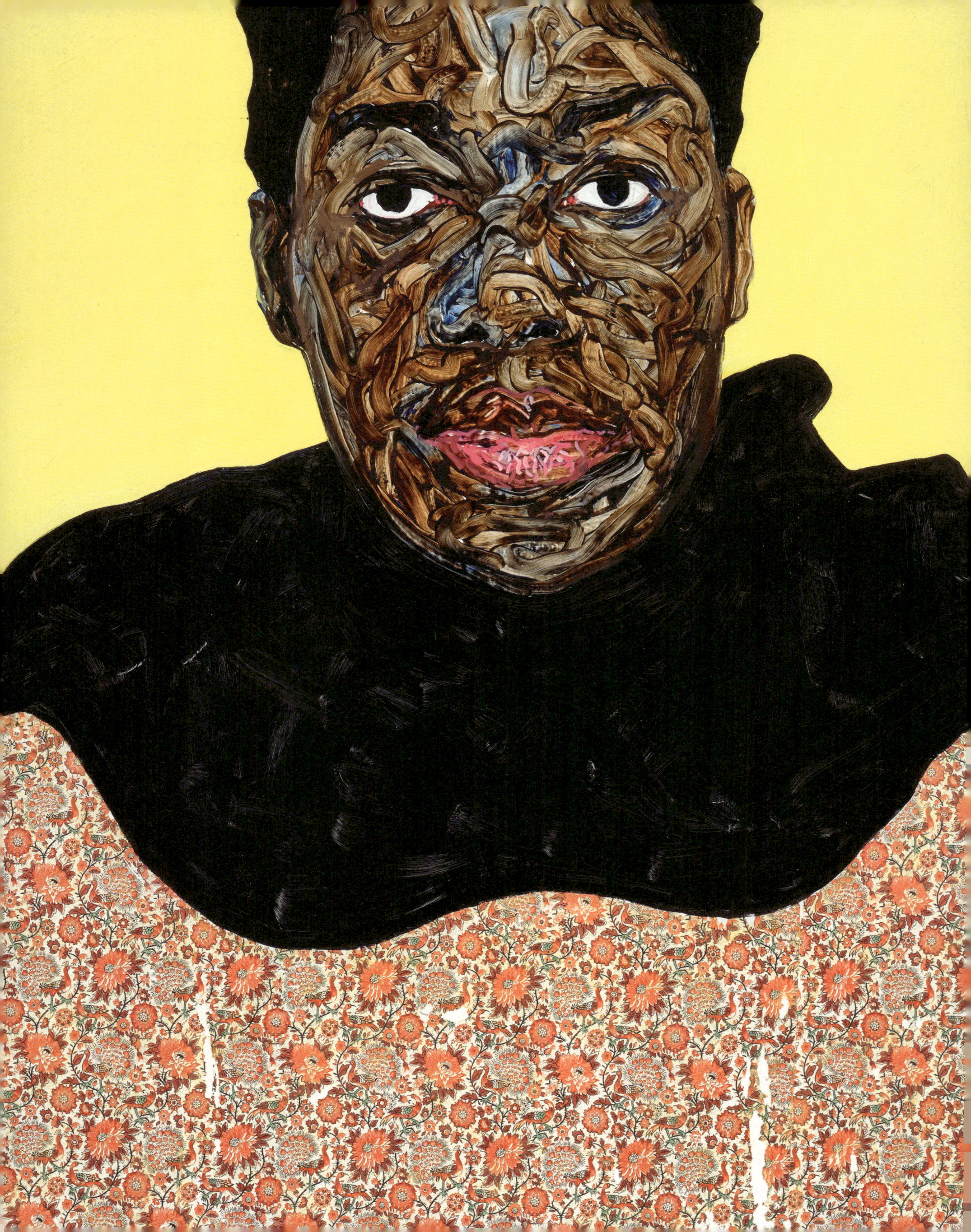

Foreword
Stella Rollig

It all started with a sentence that says more about those who asked it than about the person addressed: "Why do you only paint Black people?" Amoako Boafo was first asked this question when he arrived in Austria in 2013. He was subsequently confronted by it so often that he always had a retort ready, namely that in his home country of Ghana, the skin color of the subjects he portrayed had never been an issue.

This anecdote says a lot about the predominantly white art world of the West. It exposes the dubious self-understanding and the arrogance with which, even now, people view art and artists from places other than the Western art centers. Boafo takes the racist question and uses it as the content of one of his paintings (p. 150), which is itself included in his largest museum exhibition to date. In terms of its design, the image clearly differs from his other works, as in it a Black person is deliberately presented anonymously, without a face, holding up a panel on which precisely that question is stated, almost by way of accusation.

Despite the above experience, Boafo's artistic oeuvre stands out for its remarkable positivity, which derives from the artist's own view of life and is aptly expressed in the title of the exhibition: *Proper Love*. Boafo creates an image of Black identity that draws on itself and on its own culture and tradition, emphasizing the values of friendship, solidarity, and love. In other words, the artist counters the unequal treatment and discrimination by focusing on himself and on the people who inspire him. They may be friends, acquaintances, artists, or public figures who, in their respective realms, have influenced the (global) image and understanding of Blackness in society in their very own way. This form of Black subjectivity is also expressed in the appearance of the people he portrays; they look out at the viewer as self-confident individuals, confronting the beholder with precisely that direct gaze to which Black people are themselves exposed in white majority societies as an expression of a (possibly unintended) othering.

In the exhibition, the Belvedere presents more than fifty paintings that show Amoako Boafo is not only one of the most important artists of African art but also reveal the great influence of Viennese Modernism on his oeuvre. Through his careful, empathetic observation of the paintings of Gustav Klimt and Egon Schiele, during his time studying in Vienna Boafo developed a clear painterly style of his own that nevertheless contains reminiscences of these artistic role models. This aspect is highlighted in the second part of the exhibition, which is located in the Upper Belvedere Palace, where works by Boafo are integrated into the permanent exhibition of Viennese Modernism and placed in striking juxtaposition with works by Klimt and Schiele.

I would like to take this opportunity first and foremost to thank Amoako Boafo most cordially for the fruitful collaboration. Without his zest and dedication, we would never have been able to mount this ambitious exhibition project. I likewise wish to expressly thank Mariane Ibrahim Gallery, Chicago, Paris, and Mexico City, which enthusiastically and extensively supported the project from the very outset.

The exhibition was only possible thanks to the generous support of countless lenders: Solomon R. Guggenheim Museum, New York; Centre Georges Pompidou, Paris; Blenheim Art Foundation, Woodstock; Leopold Museum, Vienna; Fuhrman Family Collection, New York; Marieluise Hessel Collection, New York; Vilsmeier—Linhares Collection, Munich; Kehinde Wiley Collection, New York; Manuela Alexejew; Howard Blaustein; Eva Dichand; Éric Kayser; Rudolf Kratochwill; Fabrice Luzu; Corinne Moussong; Barbara Ruben; Bianca Stojka-Davis; Heinz Swoboda; Eve Therond; Jessica and Marco Verratti; and Daniel Xu. I am deeply grateful to all of them.

I would like to thank curator Sergey Harutoonian for the effective concept, planning, and implementation of the exhibition as well as for his essay in this catalogue in which he knowledgably contextualizes Amoako Boafo's creative output to date within contemporary academic discourse and highlights the influence Viennese Modernism has had on Boafo's art. As assistant curator, Vasilena Stoyanova provided support for the project, acting not only as an important interface in all manner of organizational aspects but also contributing content to the exhibition concept. I would like to thank art historian, curator, and author Mahret Ifeoma Kupka for her essay in which she considers Boafo's paintings from the viewpoint of fashion and places them in an art-sociological context with regard to the representational traditions of African photography. My thanks go to Ekow Eshun, writer and curator of trailblazing exhibitions of Black artists and the African diaspora, for his interview with Amoako Boafo, which offers deep insights into the artist's oeuvre. In her essay, author and photographer Taiye Selasi takes an historical angle on Boafo's works and his output during his time in Vienna.

My thanks go to Benjamin Buchegger and Oliver Hofmann at Studio Beton for the glorious book design and to Beba Pikall-Kotyza for coordinating the production of the catalogue. Tas Skorupa handled the editing, Dominique Haensell the sensitivity reading, and Jeremy Gaines the translations. The high-quality photographic documentation of the exhibition was, as so often, provided by Johannes Stoll. I am grateful to Leni Charles of Kids of the Diaspora for her persuasive exhibition graphics concept and the high-grade merchandise. I am indebted to Tatjana Gawron-Deutsch in our Exhibition Management section for her precise planning and coordination, and to architects Glenn DeRoché and Juergen Strohmayer for the concept and implementation of the Volta Pavilion. Finally, I would like to express my gratitude to the Art Mediation section, specifically to Kerstin Krenn, Julia Haimburger, Philipp Reichel-Neuwirth, and Katalin Várdai, to the Communications and Marketing, Restoration, Shop, and Ticketing sections, in particular to Magdalena Ruggenthaler, and to all Belvedere staff members whose dedication and effort have made this exhibition possible.

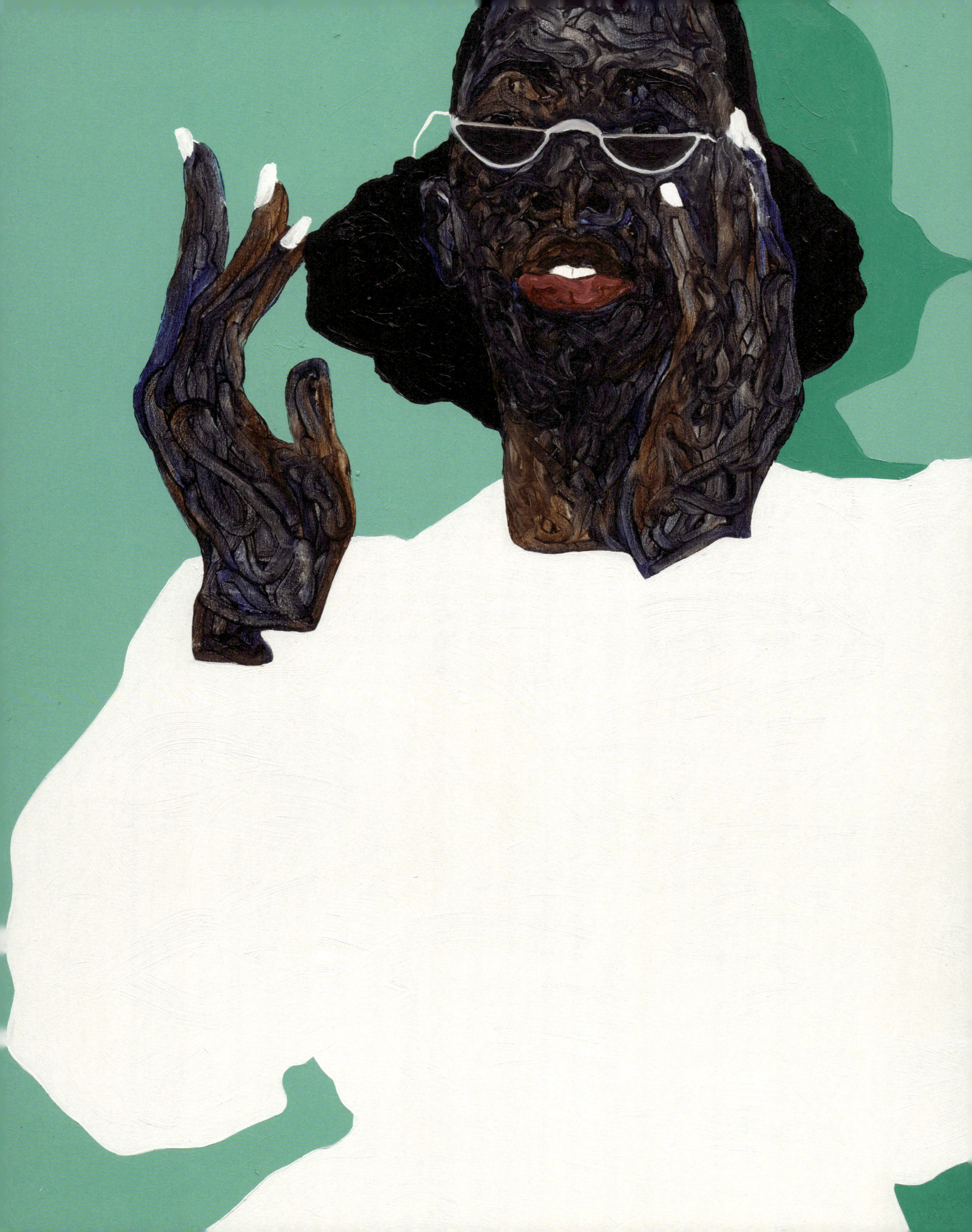

The Pictures Look at Us

How Amoako Boafo Has Shaped Current Notions and the Social Perception of Black Identity

Sergey Harutoonian

The paintings are not talking, but they are talking.
Amoako Boafo

The opening of the *Proper Love* exhibition takes place eleven years after Amoako Boafo (born in 1984 in Accra) left his home in Ghana and moved to Vienna, where he later studied painting at the Academy of Fine Arts. Those eleven years could not have been more incisive for the then unknown artist. Boafo had already obtained a degree in art in Accra, where he had studied the fundamentals of painting at the Ghanatta College of Art and Design, learning not only all about its technical implementation but also about color theories and, on graduation in 2008, receiving the accolade of "Best Portrait Painter of the Year." When he arrived in Vienna in 2013, he was already a trained painter—albeit still one in search of his own personal style.

Together with artist and curator Sunanda Mesquita, Boafo founded an initiative called WE DEY x space in Vienna,[1] which offered a presentation space to artists who had been discriminated against in the established exhibition circuit owing to their sexual orientation or gender, and who had few if any opportunities to display their art. WE DEY x space offered a safe space in which there would certainly be no ostracization, let alone exoticization of the artists.[2] The idea was to create a place for marginalized voices to be heard, voices that were otherwise ignored or squeezed out of the mainstream. Boafo was himself one of those artists who experienced discrimination, having faced the rejection of his paintings on more than one occasion when he was told,

for example, that "we don't exhibit the art of Black or African artists"[3]—a clear racist reference to his Ghanaian origins and to his images, which take the Black body as their subject matter.

These introductory biographical remarks say a lot about Amoako Boafo's experience in the Viennese exhibition world and a lot more about the constructive manner in which he has tackled rejection and animosity, as is evidenced in his artistic focus on himself and on the community of marginalized groups. This kind of self-empowerment runs like a common thread through Boafo's oeuvre. It is, in a way, a remarkable inversion of the negativity he experienced, which he has transformed into a positive focus on his own artistic work. Seen thus, the people he paints in his portraits are not only symbolic of a new Black self-confidence but also always reflect a part of his own personality—or as Boafo himself puts it far more poignantly: "I want to paint people who have had the same experiences as me. I want to see myself and have people see themselves in me."[4] The exhibition title *Proper Love* can therefore certainly be read ambivalently, as precisely his time in Vienna involved more than just positive experiences.[5]

The Belvedere has brought together over fifty works for the exhibition, and they impressively document Amoako Boafo's artistic output to date, from his artistic beginnings through to the portraits, realized in the preferred technique of finger painting for which he became known. Alongside the presentation in the Lower Belvedere Palace, the artist has integrated three of his paintings into the section of the Upper Belvedere Palace devoted to the permanent exhibition of Viennese Modernism, resulting in striking juxtapositions with key pieces by Gustav Klimt and Egon Schiele. Both artists emphatically influenced Boafo's own work. Seen from this angle, the exhibition at the Belvedere is a stroke of good fortune, as the museum possesses important collections of works by both Klimt and Schiele.

The Artist Engages in Self-Enquiry

The earliest works in the exhibition date from 2016, when Amoako Boafo studied painting at the Academy of Fine Arts Vienna. Many of the paintings he produced at this time have the artist himself as their subject matter, in part represented in the nude in intimate moments in the studio. With their calm composition, these self-portraits are politically charged, as they can also be read as direct responses to the art market's rejection of both his paintings and, in an involved, indirect manner, of his African roots. In particular, the highly dubious Western appropriation of the Black body is something Boafo explores in his paintings, such as *Reflection II* (p. 147), which shows the artist sitting in a corner of his studio on a Thonet chair. Seen from the side, Boafo is gazing into a mirror that is positioned on his radiator in such a way that the mirror image is directed straight at the viewer. The painting toys with the gaze. Intrinsic to the image is the artist himself, who seems to be carefully scrutinizing his own body in order to then establish direct eye contact with the viewer through the frontal mirror reflection. Viewers are confronted with an ambivalent gaze: while the artist shares a moment of intimacy with us, the vulnerability represented is also an attempt to counter the stereotypical image of the hypersexualized Black male body in the Global North.[6]

Boafo continued to explore this topic in his *Body Politics* and *Detoxing Masculinity* series, both made in the period between 2016 and 2018. What catches the eye is one central issue that unites many of the images: the artist reading. Boafo repeatedly portrays himself in the nude, immersed in reading books that point to a preoccupation with postcolonial and contemporary literature, including the writings of Afro-Caribbean psychiatrist, philosopher, and central pioneer of postcolonialism Frantz Fanon (1925–1961, fig. 1). The titles of the theoretical works are in part revealed by the picture titles, such as *Black Skin, White Mask* (p. 133), or are mentioned in the painting *Body Politics 2* (fig. 2). The critical exploration of toxic masculinity is expressed in pieces such as *Me, Me, and Me* (p. 143), which shows the artist in triplicate with a rose, like three muses. It is almost as if three different aspects of his personality were on display, with the element linking them highlighted by the rose as being (self-)love. Another work from the same year shows the artist in a practically lascivious, androgynous vein looking straight out of the canvas and seeking direct eye contact with viewers (*Blue Band*, p. 145).

In a certain respect, these early works already preempt Boafo's later style, even if the artist increasingly abandoned academic, realistic representation (and thus in a sense a kind of control) in favor of an experimental *non finito*—something reflected most clearly in *Yellow Blanket* (p. 137), which in several regards constitutes a key moment in Boafo's career. Here we can discern the characteristic finger painting that Boafo uses to mold his own body almost sculpturally but using the medium of painting. The surrounding space is only intimated rudimentarily; a flat yellow surface beneath the body alludes to the blanket, for example, on which the artist seems to lie.

These early works are remarkable in many respects, as they document Boafo's efforts to counter the stereotypical objectification of the Black body in paintings that offer a more differentiated image of Black identity and Black consciousness. This wish for a multifaceted representation of himself is expressed in the playful simultaneity of intellectuality and corporeality—as the outcome of artistic self-determination and not the diktat of a racist view from the outside. It is precisely here that we can detect clear references to precursors in art history, such as Édouard Manet's *Olympia* (fig. 3), of which *Yellow Blanket* could be the inverted, updated version. In the Manet, the Black body of an anonymous female servant is consigned to the margins, but Boafo places the Black male firmly in the center of the image in the place of the white female in Manet's painting.

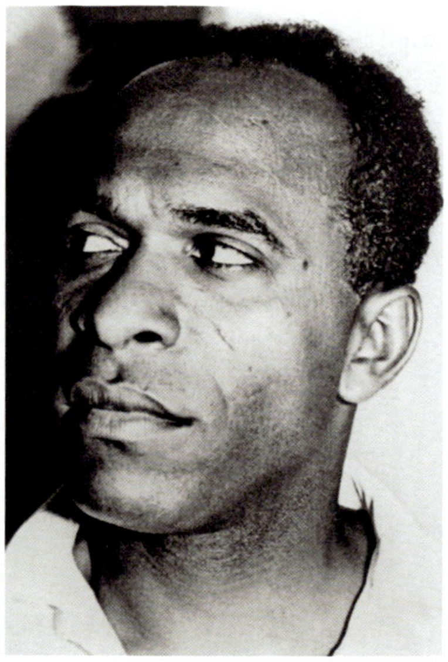

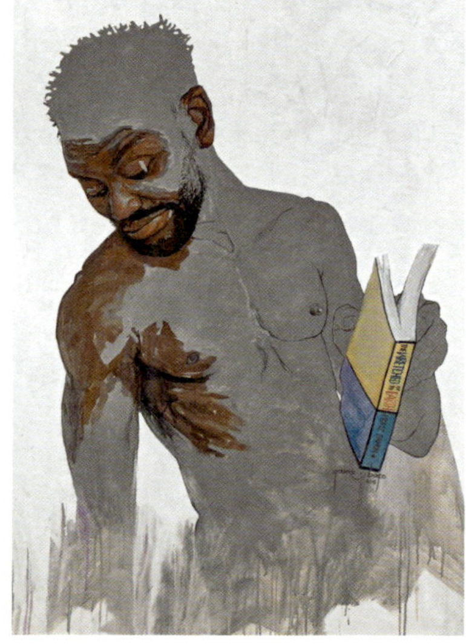

Fig. 1
Frantz Fanon, c. 1960

Fig. 2
Amoako Boafo, *Body Politics 2*, 2016
Private collection, courtesy Sotheby's

The Answering Gaze

Alongside these painterly self-observations, Amoako Boafo started
producing portraits of friends and acquaintances from the Black
community in Vienna, either working with them directly in his
studio or relying on photos sent to him. What is striking
is the reduced color palette, which is limited almost exclusively
to earthen hues or delicate pastel tones, interrupted only by
individual intense highlights of color. Boafo's enquiry into his
experience of life in Vienna prompted him to embark on this
series, entitled *Black Diaspora*, which addresses issues relating to
origin, foreignness, and identity. The pictures in the series exhibit
Boafo's typical painting style and his extreme reduction of the
composition. The bodies of those portrayed sometimes stand out
sharply against a monochrome background, the abstract qualities
of which bring to mind memories of Color Field painting.
What is striking is the way the subjects present themselves, at eye
level with the viewer and confidently seeking eye contact. The
emphasis on the gaze can also be seen from the artistic decision
to consistently portray the subjects as bust portraits: nothing
is meant to interfere with the encounter the artist seeks to foster
between the viewer and the person portrayed. A prime example
of this is *Looking Through Two Fingers* (p. 51), which shows a young
woman with short hair in three-quarter profile. Her white vest
melds smoothly with the white background so that the visible
sections of her body contrast all the more strongly. She holds her
right hand in front of her face and gazes at the viewer through
two fingers.

These images reveal very clearly Boafo's interests in his
portraits: seeing, viewing, staring—or, rather, being stared at—
perceiving and being perceived, depending on the position of the
viewer, each with a completely different intention and effect.[7]
While in a white-dominated society it is usually Black people and
people of color who get looked at, stared at, or viewed critically
primarily by white people, what we witness here is the power
relations essentially being reversed. The people portrayed by Boafo
return the gaze not only very self-confidently, but also undermine
the customary direction of the eyes so that the viewers in the
exhibition space now find themselves in the role of those being
gazed at.

Viennese Women

As mentioned, Amoako Boafo's time studying in Vienna is one
of the periods that influenced him most in artistic terms. A very
important part of this was his interaction with artists in the
Black community, who through their individual activities created
a greater visibility for people of color and Black people within
Austrian society. It was this incisive experience that affirmed
Boafo in his decision to focus his painting first and foremost on
people with black skin. The chapter of the exhibition entitled
"Viennese Women" demonstrates this with a prime selection of
portraits of well-known Viennese female artists. Boafo's method
of capturing the personality and character of his subjects is lent an
additional art-historical and sociocultural level of meaning: The
subjects portrayed include internationally exhibited artist, author,
and academic Belinda Kazeem-Kamiński (p. 65), photographer
Abiona Esther Ojo (p. 67), and musician Enyonam Tetteh-Klu
(p. 45). The artist did not choose the topic of Viennese women
by chance, as in Austrian art history in particular it is a theme
often primarily associated with Gustav Klimt's famous portraits.
In this context, the figures Boafo depicts not only reflect Vienna's
cultural world but also offer a differentiated, contemporary
picture of Austrian society. In painterly terms, we can discern
obvious parallels with Klimt's famous portraits of women in the
Belvedere's collection. In the exhibition, the paintings *Johanna*

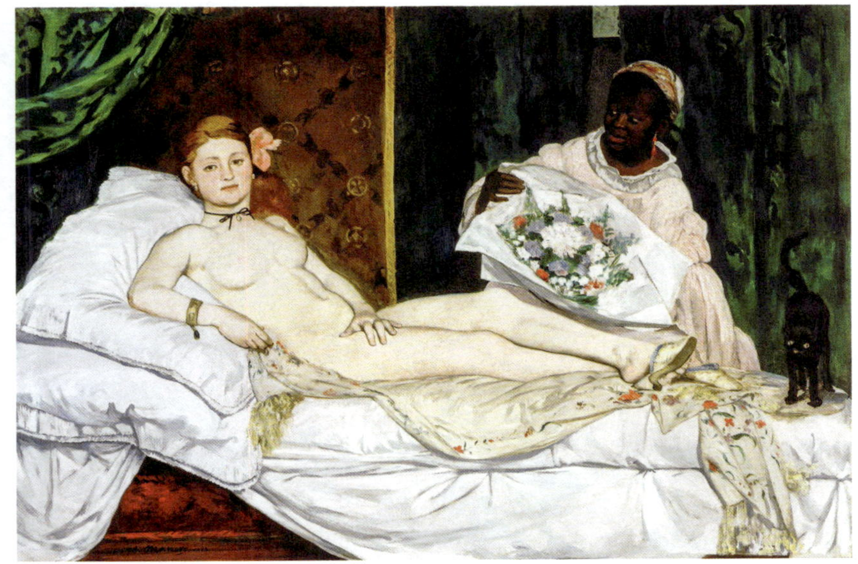

Fig. 3
Édouard Manet, *Olympia*, 1863,
Musée d'Orsay, Paris

Staude (p. 42) and *Amalie Zuckerkandl* (p. 62) are included to highlight the way Klimt's strict compositional frontality and use of ornamentation is reflected in Boafo's work. Boafo applies the chosen wallpaper pattern not directly but transposes it by means of a wet process onto the canvas, where it is used deliberately for the design of articles of clothing and accessories, creating a clear contrast to the expressive painting of the visible parts of the body. The abovementioned recurrent stylistic strategy of the *non finito* in works such as *Yellow Blanket* seems almost to have its precursor in art history in the form of the portrait of *Amalie Zuckerkandl*. In addition to the painterly references, this contrast reveals the sociopolitical dimension alluded to above, specifically if, when viewing the works, one asks the fundamental question of what it means to be an Austrian today, and to what extent artistic positions by people with an international biography are echoed in institutions of the Global North.

Proper Love

In the most extensive section of the exhibition, Amoako Boafo addresses the topic of love in its different forms and interpretations, as self-love, as interpersonal love, as love of his artistic craft, and not least as his own Black identity. The latter is the central theme here, as the artist himself emphasizes: "The primary idea of my practice is representation, documenting, celebrating, and showing new ways to approach Blackness."[8]

The paintings are in part produced using strident colors and attest to a new understanding that develops its power from within itself. They highlight a contemporary notion of Black identity that has liberated itself from that sociological phenomenon of "double consciousness" that American sociologist, writer, pan-Africanist, and socialist W. E. B. Du Bois (1868–1963, fig. 4) described in his pioneering work on the *Souls of Black Folk* (1903)

as regards the Black diaspora.[9] Du Bois used the term to capture the feeling that, as a Black person in a Western society, one was constantly perceiving oneself through the eyes of other (white) citizens and in the worst possible case oneself adopting a racist worldview. Fatally, this also leads to racist ascriptions, stereotypes, and denigrations being accepted as the norm and transposed onto oneself. Boafo's images are counterproposals to this "double consciousness" and at the same time emancipatory acts of self-determination expressed in particular through fashion and clothing. As regards his own person, Boafo comments on this form of self-determination as follows: "I didn't want to do works that complain. I wanted to do works that suggest how I want you to see me. I understand the box that you've given me, but then I also want you to know that I am much bigger than the box that you've given me."[10]

Volta Pavilion

For his exhibition at the Belvedere, Amoako Boafo has teamed up with architects DeRoché Strohmayer to create his very first site-specific installation (p. 98). The piece is reminiscent of a wooden pavilion whose construction materials originated in Lake Volta in Ghana; its comparatively modest appearance is in extreme contrast to the glorious setting of the Marble Hall. At a time when there is growing awareness of the deforestation of our planet and the related impact on the environment, Boafo has consciously chosen a material from the bottom of Lake Volta, where underwater forests resulted when the reservoir was first established. A few years ago the Ghanian government approved the removal and sale of the hardwood there, which now constitutes one of the world's largest stores of wood, for both local use and exportation.

The interior of the pavilion houses Boafo's painting *Papillon Hug* (p. 99); it depicts two women with their eyes closed in close embrace and is a central picture in the *Proper Love* exhibition. The butterflies from which the painting takes its name decorate the clothing of both women and were transposed from a paper pattern onto the canvas by a printing technique. Unlike most of his paintings, here Boafo makes use of a color for the background of the picture that does not contrast sharply with the foreground as it otherwise does in his oeuvre; the opposite is the case. The two women represented largely dissolve into the dark-brown

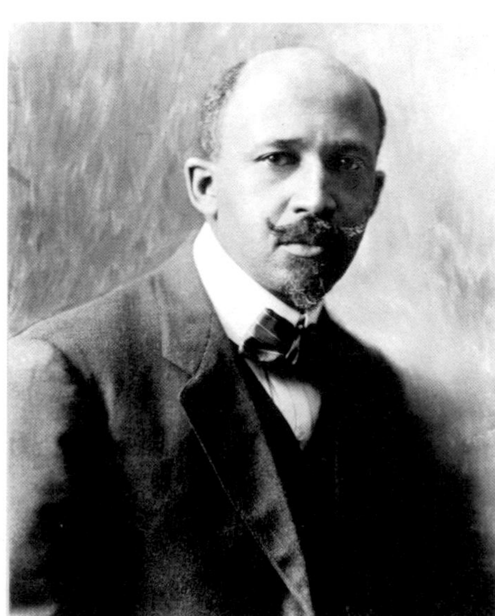

Fig. 4
William Edward Burghardt (W. E. B.) Du Bois, 1919

background, and one gets the impression that the painting and the exhibition space meld to form a unity due to this use of almost identical colors. In a gentle way, Boafo creates a space for contemplation and tranquility with this installation, encouraging an intimate dialogue between the work and the viewer. The pavilion functions accordingly as a symbol for his home country and origins while also forming a protective cocoon for the painting. By consciously alluding to Gustav Klimt's *The Kiss* (fig. 5), the painting at the same time references the Upper Belvedere, where the second part of Amoako Boafo's exhibition is to be found. In this regard, the installation and the painting have twin tasks: they offer an opportunity to pause for a moment while referring to the surrounding space outside the pavilion.

Masculinities

Amoako Boafo's critical preoccupation with and exploration of stereotypical images of masculinity can already be seen in his self-portraits, when he repeatedly paints himself in contrived poses (*Self Portrait—Blue Band and Pink Hair*, fig. 6), with painted fingernails, or in the nude (*Me, Me, and Me*, p. 143)—poses that in art history tend to be associated with traditions of depicting women.

In conversation with art historian Paul Schimmel, Boafo explained his differentiated approach in detail: "In Ghana, as a man, you are supposed to show strength by being aggressive. And to show a sign of softness—people assume that you are gay. And I, of course, didn't get it, but I still don't get it. Why can't I paint my nails or wear earrings or a nose ring and still be masculine? I thought about it then, but I didn't know how to address it. But when I moved to Vienna, I had enough time to think about it and to just dive into it. And it was just for me to tell myself, 'It's okay, I can wear nail polish. I can put on earrings and a nose ring and

be masculine. I don't have to be aggressive. I don't have to punch someone to show strength.'"[11]

This staging of himself in particular and of the male body in general clearly has parallels with Egon Schiele's self-portraits (fig. 7), which in a similar way exude a sense of the androgenous and vulnerability and run counter to the stereotypical image of masculinity. That said, there are also elements of playful coexistence (*Mr. Palm with the Yellow Ball*, p. 111), of relaxed leisure time (*Strawberries and Pink Shorts*, p. 119), and of fashionable self-representation (*Pink Hat*, p. 107) that attest to Boafo's efforts to offer a differentiated depiction of masculinity. This is incisively shown in his *Detoxing Masculinity* exhibition, held at the Vienna off-space WE DEY x space in 2017, where he presented several of his self-portraits on this theme (*Gold Leaves*, p. 141).[12]

The topic is reflected in this section of the exhibition in a further juxtaposition, where a Boafo painting inspired by American artist Jean-Michel Basquiat (1960–1988, p. 117) is juxtaposed with Egon Schiele's portrait of *Eduard Kosmack* (p. 114). In the two images, which have astonishing parallels in terms of the structure, colors, and representation of the human body, the viewer will encounter two diametrically opposed notions of masculinity. Boafo stages Basquiat as a self-confident libertine, who, with a casual glance and an outsized jacket, represents a modern notion of masculinity beyond all patriarchal gestures of dominance, while Schiele, in his portrait of Eduard Kosmack, emphasizes the publisher's inaccessible nature. The encounter with the represented person, with his piercing, almost hypnotic gaze and dismissive posture, is tantamount to a confrontation.

Before his breakthrough in the international art scene, Amoako Boafo was repeatedly asked why he only painted Black people, given that representations of white people would definitely sell better. In the final gallery in the exhibition, Boafo displays his painting *Why Do You Only Paint Black People* (p. 150), which cannot be readily categorized for several reasons and can be read as a direct response to that question: the person portrayed has no face; the figure is only a vague outline and seems almost to dissolve into the dark background. Here there is no eye contact, otherwise a characteristic feature of almost all of Boafo's paintings. It can only be surmised that the person portrayed is the artist himself, represented in a white shirt with colored dots and with turquoise-colored fingernails and hair. He holds a panel

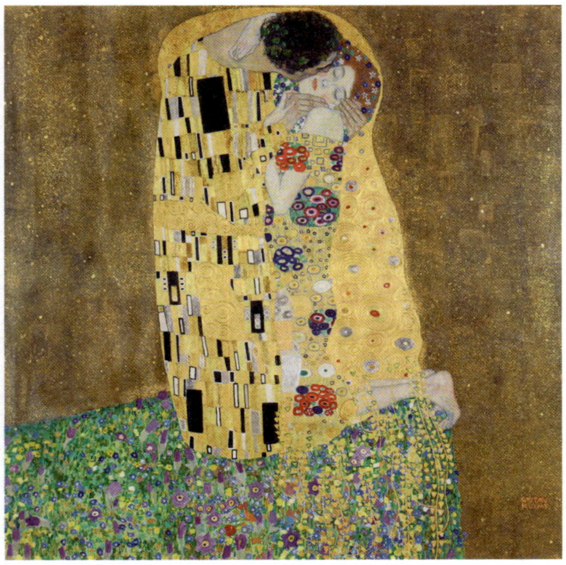

Fig. 5
The Kiss (Lovers), 1908 (completed 1909)
Belvedere, Vienna

up in front of his chest asking the question stated in the title. The
question mark at the end has been omitted, so that the statement
the work makes remains ambiguous: is the artist repeating the
question he was so often asked, or is it rather a statement by him
with which he is now confronting viewers? The word *BLACK*
written in red seems to be emphasized, and the color that thus
departs from the meaning of the word underscores the absurdity
of the question and how constructed the notion "black" is, since,
taken precisely, it does not refer to a color at all.

Boafo presents by way of a final image a painting that makes
an unambiguous statement and is ostensibly meant to be received
by the Western art world, whose standards, until recently, Black
artists and people of color simply had to comply with. This is
the conclusion that Boafo offers viewers at the end of the exhibition, and it is up to them what answer they find to the question
asked, or whether they even need to answer it. Seen from this
viewpoint, too, Boafo's career as outlined above is remarkable: in
the absence of access to sources on art history and art theory,
in his early years Boafo focused entirely on the medium of painting
and the immediate lived reality of his fellow Black citizens and
his friends as his subject matter. On this basis, he saw all the
more clearly the everyday discrimination of Black positions of the
African diaspora in Western societies, and convincingly responded
to them through his oeuvre. His are paintings that tell not only
of artistic self-empowerment and self-discovery, but also of the
changed self-perception of Black people. The artist himself and his
view of the world are a key part of this.

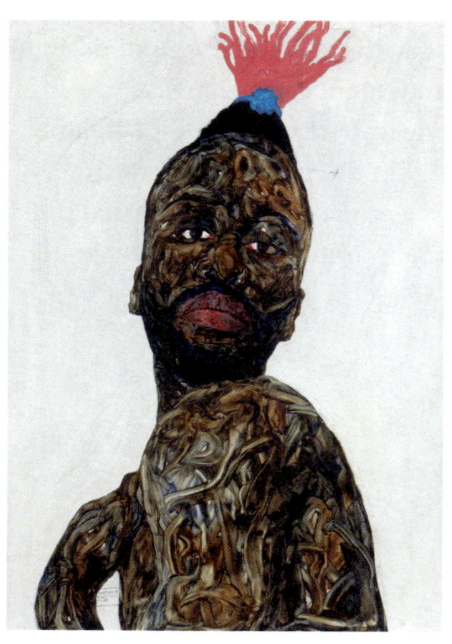

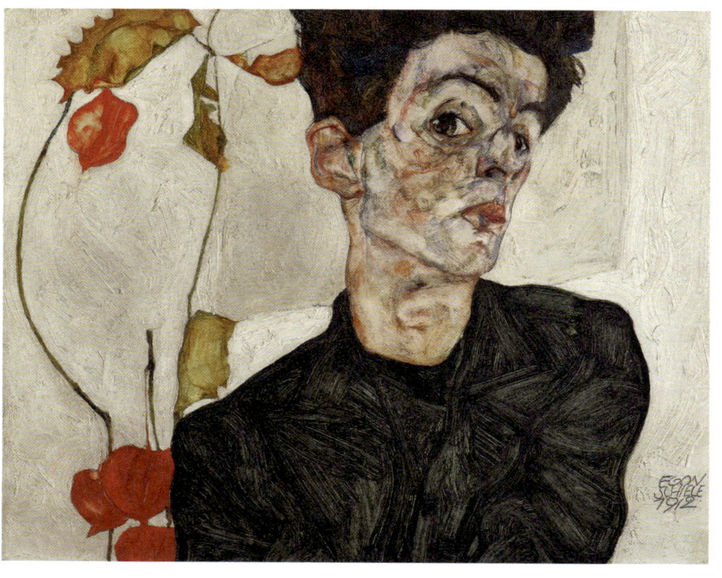

Fig. 6
Amoako Boafo, *Self Portrait—
Blue Band and Pink Hair*, 2019
Courtesy Amoako Boafo
and Roberts Projects, Los Angeles

Fig. 7
Egon Schiele, *Self-Portrait
with Chinese Lantern Plant*, 1912
Leopold Museum, Vienna

1 The term *we dey* derives from Pidgin English and can be loosely translated as "we are." Pidgin is based on appropriating the colonial language of English and is spoken in former British colonies such as Ghana and Nigeria as well as by the West African diaspora on the continent and beyond. See "We Dey x Space" on https://blackpeopleinvienna.com /organizations/we_dey_x_space (accessed on July 16, 2024).

2 Paul Schimmel, "Painting Is a Safe Refuge: An Interview with Amoako Boafo," in *Amoako Boafo*, ed. Roberts Projects (Los Angeles, 2022), p. 25.

3 Schimmel 2022 (see note 2), p. 26.

4 Quoted from Osei Bonsu, ed., *African Art Now: Fifty Pioneers Defining African Art for the Twenty-First Century* (London, 2022), p. 53.

5 On this, see the conversation between Amoako Boafo and Ekow Eshun in this catalogue, p. 27.

6 On this, see the conversation between Boafo and Eshun in this catalogue, p. 26.

7 Larry Ossei-Mensah, "An Artist's Gaze," in *Amoako Boafo: Soul of Black Folks*, ed. Larry Ossei-Mensah, exh. cat. Denver Art Museum & Contemporary Arts Museum Houston (Petaluma, CA, 2023), p. 18.

8 This quote originated from a conversation between the author and the artist.

9 Richard J. Powell, "Les âmes illustrées: W. E. B. Du Bois dans l'art contemporain," in *The Colour Line: Les Artistes africains-américains et la ségrégation, 1865–1916*, ed. Daniel Soutif, exh. cat. Musée Quai Branly, Paris (Paris, 2017), p. 77.

10 Amoako Boafo in conversation with Ekow Eshun in this catalogue, p. 26.

11 Schimmel 2022 (see note 2), p. 24.

12 Schimmel 2022 (see note 2), p. 25.

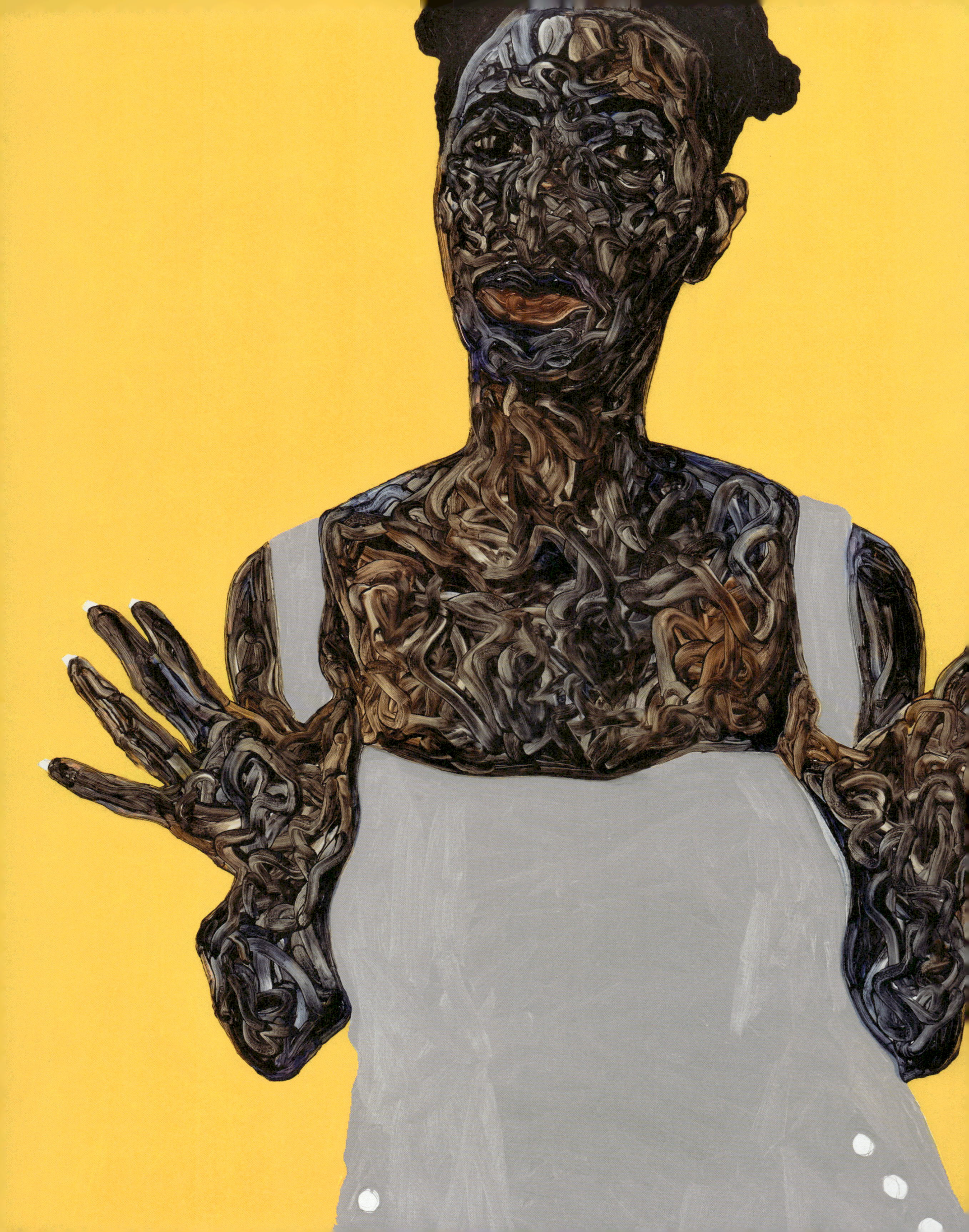

Style Narratives of
Black Self-Empowerment

On the Significance of Clothing
in Amoako Boafo's Portraits

Mahret Ifeoma Kupka

The two paintings I have chosen as the starting point for my remarks on the significance of fashion and clothing in the portraits by Amoako Boafo[1] are both of Thelma Golden, who is the director of the Studio Museum in Harlem, New York. In an interview, the artist recalled how he briefly met her on his first visit to the institution: "On my way out, I saw her coming in with this big smile on her face."[2] It captivated him, and back in Vienna, where he lived at the time and was studying at the Academy of Fine Arts, he started painting several portraits from memory and also relying on photos from the internet. "I wasn't in the position to ask her to take a picture. So, I went online and started taking images from photos where she was wearing things that I liked. And then from there, I did a couple of paintings of her."[3] One of them is entitled *Red Dress* (fig. 1). Golden is depicted sitting on a red couch, one leg crossed over the other. The red of the sofa, against a gray background, is only slightly darker than the red of the titular long dress (with green, blue, and white dots), which reveals part of one leg. Dress and sofa almost meld to form a single shimmering surface. With her head resting on her fist and her elbow on the arm of the sofa, she gazes contemplatively into the distance, out of the pictorial space, and thus differs from most of Boafo's models, who tend to look directly into the viewer's eyes. Her right hand rests next to her on the seat. "I draw strength and inspiration from the community," is how Boafo explains the choice of theme in another interview. "I very much like people who create space for other people to exist and Thelma happens to be one of them."[4]

Thelma Golden's shows at the Studio Museum in Harlem[5] have repeatedly created a space for considering the influence of structural, social conditions on artistic practices. What roles do categories such as race play? What does it mean to be a Black artist in a world dominated by whiteness? How does the meaning of Blackness[6] change in a world that becomes ever more differentiated?[7] These are questions that are also expressed artistically in Boafo's portraits of exclusively Black persons.

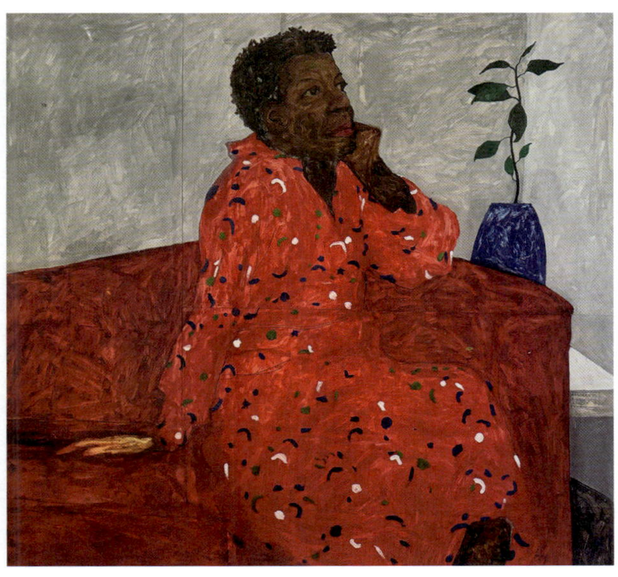

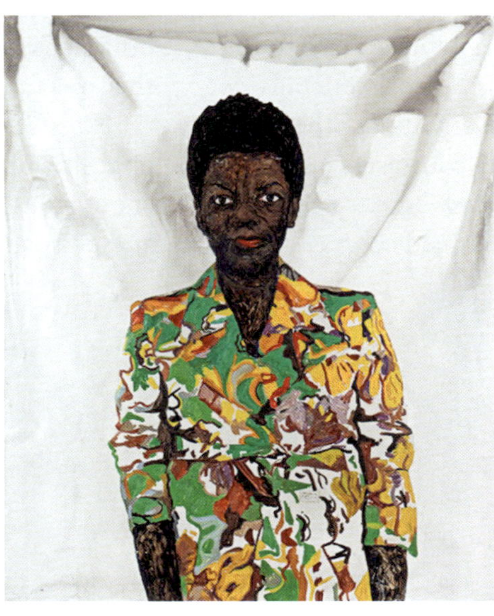

Fig. 1
Amoako Boafo, *Red Dress*, 2017
Jesse Williams Collection

Fig. 2
Amoako Boafo,
Thelma in Colored Blazer, 2018

17

Another portrait presents Golden in a colorfully patterned, tapered blazer. Her gaze is directed, a touch suspiciously, at the viewer. She has seemingly casually pulled up the arms of her jacket, leaving her lower arms exposed; she is pressing them into her tense body. The background resembles some provisionally hung sheet or an empty canvas left off its stretcher. The picture's dynamics focus on the pattern of her clothing. *Thelma in Colored Blazer* (fig. 2) presents vibrant green, red, and yellow shapes and surfaces that interweave as if in dance. The focus is on the woman portrayed and her blazer, which is not only a piece of clothing in its most fundamental, pragmatic function (as a way of covering the body) or decoration but in fact becomes a central style element in the painting. Who is actually wearing whom here, a viewer might ask. Borrowing on the definition given by design theorist Carol Tulloch, style can be understood here as a way of constructing the self, as self-styling, by the way you arrange your articles of clothing, accessories, and choose your hairdo. In this case it is Golden's characteristic short haircut and her makeup, including her strikingly red lipstick.[8] For Tulloch, style is part of a "process of self-telling," in which the individual develops through their own style. The conscious choice of clothing forms a narrative of its own, a "style narrative" as Tulloch calls it.[9] *Thelma in Colored Blazer* shows a woman who self-confidently appropriates the body and space that she inhabits. The colorful blazer becomes an extension of herself.[10]

Making this "style narrative" his own is doubtless part of Boafo's artistic license. It is not the persons portrayed who express themselves through their choice of clothes, but the artist who styles his models on canvas. Sometimes it is only a detail that he has observed (an accessory, red fingernail polish, a specific hairdo, or a hat) that later becomes a central element in a portrait. A prime example of this is *Strawberries and Pink Shorts* (p. 119), which shows a young man wearing pink shorts and a white T-shirt lying with a bowl of strawberries on a white blanket on a green lawn. The skin of the man's face, arms, and legs is molded into the canvas in Boafo's characteristic finger technique. The T-shirt and blanket flow together to form a white surface from which the head and arms protrude, blurring any other details in them. The scene is completed in the viewers' minds. The white bowl with the intimated strawberries barely contrasts with the background. Together with the red of the strawberries against the white background, the pink shorts as a color field contrast

brightly with the dark green of the grass. "Take a seat and have a strawberry," the man's soft gaze seems to say.

An early Boafo exhibition project that contextualizes *Strawberries and Pink Shorts* was called *Detoxing Masculinity*.[11] In a series of self-portraits, Boafo addressed social notions of masculinity, his own West African religious background, and racist European projections. "While disrupting the white gaze onto his naked Black body with non-stereotypical representations of Black masculinity, the series can be read as journey, longing for self-love and self-care. Black self-love is revolutionary in a world which still sees the Black male body as something to be consumed, to be hyper-sexualized and at the same time something to be afraid of," the text accompanying the show stated.[12] In an interview Boafo commented, "In Ghana, as a man, you are supposed to show strength by being aggressive. And to show a sign of softness— people assume that you are gay"[13] and by extension not masculine. By portraying himself with painted fingernails, a nose ring, or flowers, he challenges the limiting gender stereotype: "I can put on earrings and nose ring and be masculine. I don't have to be aggressive. I don't have to punch someone to show strength."[14] In Boafo's works, Black men are allowed to wear pink shorts and enjoy lying around on a lawn and munching strawberries with their partners and friends.

Christine Checinska, among other things curator of African and African diaspora fashion at the Victoria and Albert Museum in London, draws on the work of fashion theorist Susan B. Kaiser to describe the significance of clothing and fashion for the self-construction of Black masculinity and suggests "those who have been historically constructed as objects may use dress as a vehicle for subjectivity."[15] Checinska starts her discussion with an analysis of the role of clothing in the Haitian Revolution (1791–1804), which differed sharply from its function in the nearly concurrent French Revolution (1789–99). In fashion studies with a Western orientation, the revolution in Europe is often considered the starting point of modern men's fashion: "Fashions in male dress shifted from an *ancien régime* reliance on color and ornamentation, which denoted social rank, toward clothing that was functional, discrete, and suitable."[16] By contrast, from the African-Caribbean perspective, the trend went in exactly the opposite direction: "Dress changed from being the functional and anonymous (un)dress of the slaves to being elegant, embellished, and personalized, announcing the status of the wearer as free, equal, and part of the humanity of all men."[17] What fashion in France forfeited in terms of opulence during this period of the Great Male Renunciation in favor of democratization in the sense of greater equality between the estates, it gained in Haiti—or rather was able to articulate as such for the very first time there—as the "Great Masculine Enunciation," embodied by celebrities such as Jean-Jacques Dessalines. He was a man who had been enslaved in West Africa as an adolescent and emerged in 1804 as the first governor general of the independent Republic of Haiti and subsequently (until he was murdered in 1806) became emperor of the First Empire of Haiti. Busts, engravings, and paintings always depict him with a Napoleonic cocked hat with three plumes and a jacket decorated with tassels and a laurel-leaf pattern. "The Haitian Revolution and spectacle of its leaders' dress challenged eighteenth-century Western thinking about race," Checinska writes.[18] Back then, a revolution was as inconceivable as the sight of former slaves in full military regalia behaving as if they were in Versailles. It was also unimaginable because at the beginning of the Revolution Black people were legally forbidden to bear arms or wear European clothing.

When sociologist, philosopher, and journalist W. E. B. Du Bois opened *The Exhibit of American Negroes*, the show he had cocurated at the 1900 Exposition Universelle in Paris with Thomas J. Calloway, his main intention was to juxtapose images of flourishing, emancipated, educated, and free Black people in American culture with the widespread racist representations of Black people in the Western visual and popular culture of the 1890s. Among other things, the exhibition presented a statuette of abolitionist Frederick Douglass, four volumes with almost four hundred official patents held by African Americans, photographs of various educational institutions, an African American bibliography for the Library of Congress featuring 1,400 titles, and two social studies that Du Bois conducted and produced with his students at Atlanta University, consisting of handmade charts and diagrams on the African American population. In addition, there were about five hundred photographs, including countless portraits of African American men and women. Clothing played a decisive role in this context: "Many of the portrait photographs show African American women posing in fashionable styles of the time, such as fur collars or ruched blouses with high-fitting collars. With their dandyesque looks, some even seemed to transcend the 'gender' categories of that time in their clothing, wearing men's jackets, shirts, or coats in the styles of soldiers' uniforms," write fashion theorists Elke Gaugele and Monica Titton.[19] Du Bois himself arrived in Paris dressed as an "elegant African American gentleman" in black tails and top hat, staging himself as a graduate of an Ivy League university and a scholar of science and culture. "The 'Race Man's uniform,' suggested by Du Bois at that time, adopts the well-fitting Victorian three-piece suit and thus appropriates a highly symbolic piece of normative masculinity and authority."[20] This self-narrative was, similarly to the combatants in the Haitian Revolution, to become a metaphor for a modern outfit that stood for liberty, opposition, and self-empowerment within racist American society.[21]

A few years later, the style of those represented became a crucial element in the works of photographers such as Malick Sidibé (fig. 3) and James Barnor. Anyone who in the late 1940s stepped into Seydou Keïta's studio in Bamako had dressed for the event and was ready to become part of a proud narrative on a new, modern West Africa. From 1946 onwards, as of the first meeting of the Francophone Congrès de Bamako, Mali's capital city developed into an important French colonial center. The number of its inhabitants soared, there was a direct railway link to Dakar, bringing the city closer to Paris. Its market meant Bamako was likewise an important center of regional trade.[22] While racist ideologies of colonialism had categorized Africans as being subhuman and uncivilized, denying them any creative abilities, the focus now and in the age of independence from colonial rule for over seventeen West African states that immediately followed was on developing a new sense of pride in being Black and, above all, African. Art, design, and music played a part in finding contemporary forms that drew on precolonial history and at the same time referenced an African modern present and future—a cultural renaissance. "The fashions of the day both set and kept

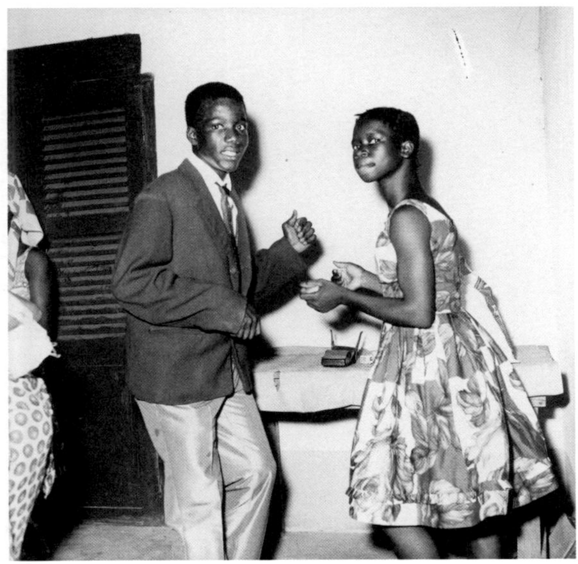

Fig. 3
Malick Sidibé, *Surprise Partie*, 1964 (printed 1998)
Solomon R. Guggenheim Museum, New York; Gift,
The Bohen Foundation, 2001, 2001.258

pace with the rhythms of freshly independent lives. The body became a site of transformation and representation, a primary symbol in the 'performances through which modernity [was] conceived, constructed and challenged in Africa'. […] The fashions worn allowed us to show ourselves to the world as we knew ourselves to be—as individuals with diverse beliefs, values, styles and identities," Checinska writes.[23]

Having your portrait taken by Keïta was a sign of cosmo-politanism and meant that the person portrayed was *modern*. There are clear parallels here to Boafo's painted portraits. Both focus on fashion details and opt for a planar representation. Their models seem to have been extracted from any direct context, from time and bereft of all individual experience, creating scope for the imagination. The persons who wanted to be *bamakois* sat, stood, or lay for Keïta like models for a painter. They always seem to be idealized, the products of the photographer and representatives of his idea of a modern Bamako. In a very similar manner, Boafo's friends and acquaintances, and people he admires usually morph not least in the titles of his portraits, such as *Silver Dungaree* (p. 75), into the nameless representatives of a higher ideal.

It is typical of portraits that they tell many stories. Those of the persons represented as well as the intention(s) of the portrayer and the context(s) in which they are respectively embedded. For Boafo, Vienna was the place where he found the time and space to experiment. While in Accra he had acquired the technique and learned the use of colors at the Ghanatta College of Art and Design, had trained to work with great precision; at the Academy of Fine Arts Vienna he had the freedom to develop his own forms and by studying originals was able to weave references to European art history into his own output.[24] At the same time, the move from Accra to Vienna brought with it the new experience of life in the diaspora, in a predominantly white society, including the experience of a changed physical presence. It also meant confronting the still smoldering remains of racist ascriptions of colonialism, the lack of representation and recognition that Boafo opposes in his portraits by self-confidently creating his own counterimages. He does not simply paint the person but captures on the canvas what the person represents for him, what meaning they have to him in a racist world that hardly provides any space for active Black self-development and in which he himself and his friends and acquaintances are forever trying to inscribe themselves. With the focus he attaches in the process to clothing, by developing his own fashions and styles, Boafo also takes his place in the history of Black self-empowerment. A specific choice of clothing, as the examples of the significance of military regalia during the Haitian Revolution, the role of clothing in the self-narrative of African American lived realities as presented by W. E. B. Du Bois at the 1900 Exposition Universelle in Paris or in Seydou Keïta's portrayal of a modern Bamako, has always had a decisive weight in positioning Black persons against violent, discriminating white narratives: "Self-fashioning can be a transformational act, a masquerade that realigns the sense of self, facilitating the decolonization of one's mind," Checinska comments, and continues, "One can achieve a freedom from societies' confounding constraints based on negative readings of racial, cultural and gendered difference."[25] The strategic design of the body, self-styling, can become a political act. Carefully chosen fabrics and fashions, be it on your own body or captured on canvas, become an integral element of the work of remembering and of self-empowerment. However, it is a process that can never come to an end: "Because of the nature of everyday racism, any such freedoms are temporary."[26] The racialized visual field and the colonial-racist eye constantly adapt and call for new forms of distinction. One solution is presumably beyond racialized categories. And that is a long path. For the meantime, Boafo has chosen his own kind of nonchalance: "I think I did a lot of painting just complaining about it. […] but now I want to make paintings to suggest how I want you to see me. I'm not going to complain anymore. I'm just going to tell you this is how I am. This is how I want you to see me."[27] Boafo gazes at us from each of his styled portraits. And we gaze back.

1 In the texts and interviews published to date on Amoako Boafo, there has always been an emphasis on the importance of fashion in his portraiture. The focus tends to be on his contribution to a changing practice of representing Black life and Black corporeality. In the present article, I concentrate on how Boafo uses fashion and clothing in his portraits as the language of self-empowerment and thus by means of clothing inscribes himself in a history of the Black community's self-narrative. While the reports on Boafo's cooperation with French fashion corporation Dior concentrate directly on fashion, I do not address this aspect here. See Olivia Singer, "'It's an Exchange': Kim Jones on His Mesmerizing Collaboration with Amoako Boafo for Dior Men SS21," *British Vogue*, July 13, 2020, https://www.vogue.co.uk/fashion/article/dior-men-spring-summer-2021 (accessed on January 28, 2024); Ryan Waddoups, "The Story behind Amoako Boafo's Deeply Personal Collection with Dior," *Surface*, July 16, 2020, https://www.surfacemag.com/articles/dior-ss21-amoako-boafo/ (accessed on January 28, 2024); and Daniel Kalt, "Amoako Boafo: Die Türen öffnen sich," *Die Presse: Schaufenster*, no. 33, November 27, 2020, pp. 12–15.

2 Quoted from Paul Schimmel, "Painting Is a Safe Refuge: An Interview with Amoako Boafo," in *Amoako Boafo*, ed. Roberts Projects (Los Angeles, 2022), p. 35.

3 Quoted from Schimmel 2022 (see note 2).

4 Quoted from Victoria L. Valentine, "Culture Talk: Amoako Boafo's First Exhibition at Roberts Projects in Los Angeles Centers Black Subjectivity," *Culture Type*, February 15, 2019, https://www.culturetype.com/2019/02/15/amoako-boafos-first-exhibition-at-roberts-projects-in-los-angeles-centers-black-subjectivity/ (accessed on January 14, 2024).

5 Four exhibitions are worthy of mention in this context and can retrospectively be grouped together as the F series: *Freestyle* (2001), *Frequency* (2005), *Flow* (2008), and *Fore* (2013).

6 I understand *Blackness* as a notion of being-in-the-world in the way the term is used, among others, by Calvin Warren, Fred Moten, Saidiya Hartman, and Stefano Harney: "Blackness designates not *only* Black people, but also conceptual existence as an ontological state, an aesthetic principle, historical suffering, and a form of thought. There are many different definitions for this word, and they are all highly dependent on context." Henrike Kohpeiss, *Bürgerliche Kälte: Affekt und koloniale Subjektivität* (Frankfurt am Main/New York, 2023), pp. 14–15.

7 Early in the first decade of the twenty-first century, together with artist Glenn Ligon, Thelma Golden coined the term *post-black* and in doing so triggered a controversial debate in art and beyond about a changing Black self-understanding. See Thelma Golden, "Introduction," in *Freestyle*, ed. Thelma Golden (New York, 2001), p. 14.

8 Carol Tulloch, "Style—Fashion—Dress: From Black to Post-Black," *Fashion Theory*, yr. 14, no. 3 (2010), p. 276.

9 As long ago as 1967 in his *Système de la mode*, which was published in English as *The Fashion System* in 1983, Roland Barthes analyzed fashion as a legible text that, embedded in a personal and collective system of communication generated its meaning in the respective context. In 1957 Erving Goffman proposed in *The Presentation of Self in Everyday Life* that all people at all times stage themselves in their everyday actions as if on a stage and create a different façade depending on the scene. The authors I cite here refer among others to these considerations but expand them to include the category of race and focus also on the experience of Black self-staging with reference to white majority societies. Distinction is something that no longer separates social classes. See Roland Barthes, *The Fashion System* (New York, 1983); Erving Goffman, *The Presentation of Self in Everyday Life* (New York, 1959); and Pierre Bourdieu, *Distinction* (London, 1984).

10 The portrait is based on a photograph from a report in the *Los Angeles Times*, which shows Thelma Golden in 2018 when being awarded the Getty Medal. In the text, the author underlines the curator's style: "Golden is small, barely cracking 5 feet, a fact that is prominently noted in just about every profile ever written about her—profiles that also never fail to mention her meticulous fashion sense. (For our interview, she materializes in a bright floral jacket and a pair of sculptural animal print sandals.)" Carolina A. Miranda, "From 125th Street in Harlem, Thelma Golden Has Changed the Face of Art All over the US," *Los Angeles Times*, September 24, 2018, https://www.latimes.com/entertainment/arts/miranda/la-et-cam-thelma-golden-wins-getty-medal-20180924-story.html (accessed on January 28, 2024).

11 The solo exhibition *Detoxing Masculinity* ran from June 22 to July 8, 2017, at WE DEY x space in Vienna.

12 Sunanda Mesquita, "Amoako Boafo Solo Exhibition," August 21, 2017, https://we-dey.in/tag/detoxing-masculinities/ (accessed on January 25, 2024).

13 Quoted from Schimmel 2022 (see note 2), p. 24.

14 Quoted from Schimmel 2022 (see note 2), p. 24.

15 Christine Checinska, "(Re-)fashioning African Diasporic Masculinities," in *Fashion and Postcolonial Critique*, eds. Elke Gaugele and Monica Titton (Berlin, 2019), p. 84; referring to Susan B. Kaiser, *The Social Psychology of Clothing* (New York, 1997), pp. 79–83.

16 Checinska 2019 (see note 15), p. 82.

17 Checinska 2019 (see note 15).

18 Checinska 2019 (see note 15), p. 84.

19 Elke Gaugele and Monica Titton, "Fashion and Postcolonial Critique: An Introduction," in *Fashion and Postcolonial Critique*, eds. Elke Gaugele and Monica Titton (Berlin, 2019), p. 23.

20 Gaugele and Titton 2019 (see note 19).

21 Fashion was also to play a key role in the American Civil Rights movement, "from the prim, tailored clothing of the 1950s to the African-inspired print of the Black Arts movement of the 1960s to the militant black turtlenecks and denim of the Black Panther Party of the 1970s. The aesthetics of the civil rights movement spread the message of Black pride and resistance to the masses even more so than pamphlets and speeches." Angela Tate, "Fashioning the Protest," *The Fashion and Race Database*, April 6, 2022, https://fashionandrace.org/database/fashioning-the-protest/ (accessed on January 28, 2024).

22 Manthia Diawara, "Talk of the Town: Seydou Keïta," *Artforum*, yr. 36, no. 6 (February 1998), https://www.artforum.com/features/talk-of-the-town-seydou-keita-2-201629/ (accessed on January 28, 2024).

23 Christine Checinska, "The Politics of Fabric and Fashion in Africa 1960—Today," lecture at Gresham College, October 20, 2022, https://www.gresham.ac.uk/watch-now/africa-fashion (accessed on January 28, 2024).

24 Kalt 2020 (see note 1), p. 13; and Osei Bonsu, "The Mirror's Edge," in *Amoako Boafo*, ed. Roberts Projects (Los Angeles, 2022), p. 12.

25 Checinska 2022 (see note 23).

26 Checinska 2019 (see note 15), p. 87.

27 Quoted from Schimmel 2022 (see note 2), pp. 25–26.

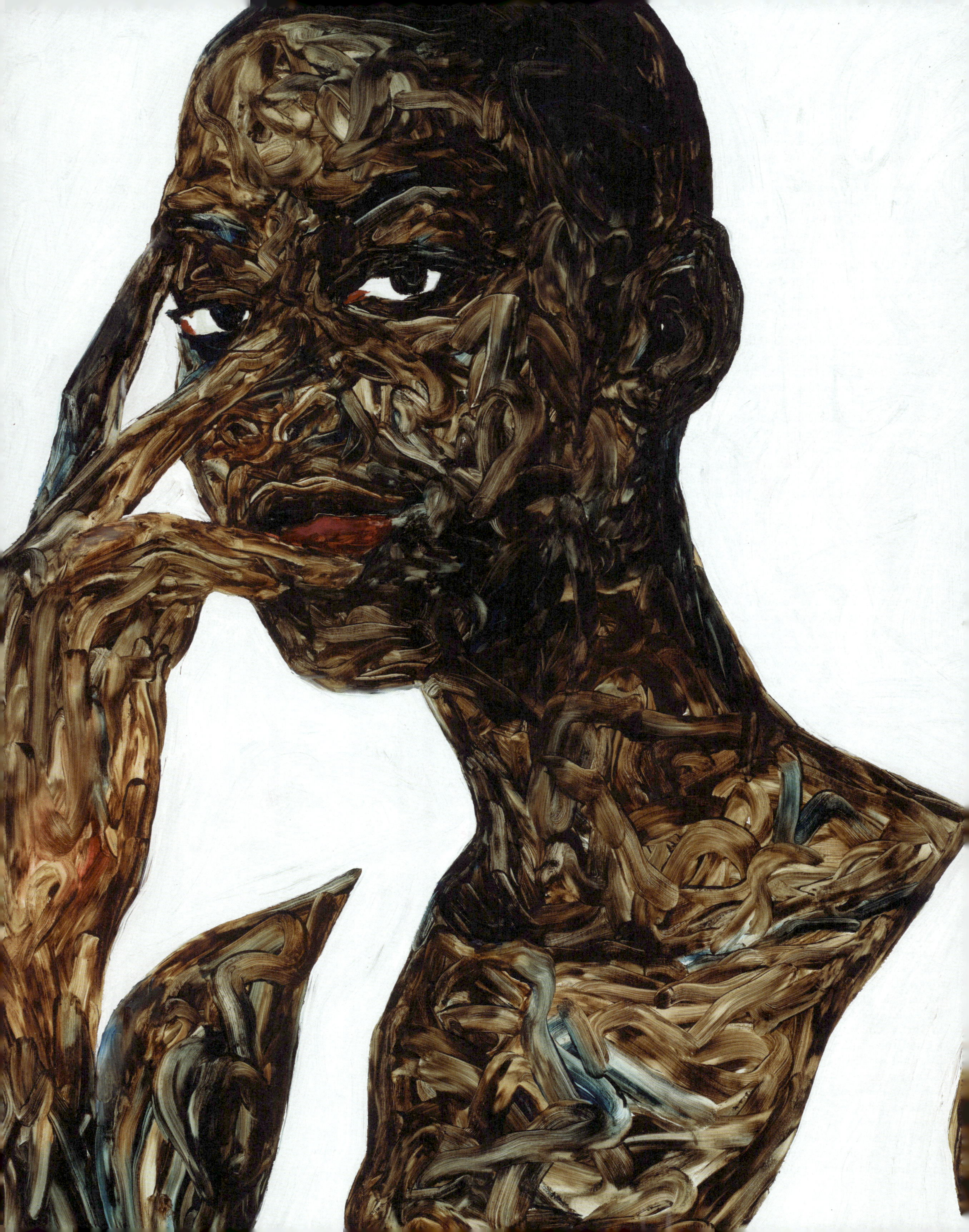

Ekow Eshun in Conversation with Amoako Boafo

Ekow Eshun   I'd like to start by going back to your arrival in Vienna in 2013 and what kind of experience that was. What were you looking for and what did you find when you arrived in Vienna?

Amoako Boafo   I had a chance because Sunanda [Mesquita] managed to get me a show in Vienna with an art space called Fortuna Galerie. It was a way for me to get to see Vienna and decide if it was a place where I would like to stay. It was just an introduction, a way to introduce Vienna to me. So we organized a small exhibition—I mean, now I'm saying small, but it was big!

EE   How many pieces were in the show at that time?

AB   I don't remember, but more than ten pieces. It was quite cold, and it was my first time traveling outside of Accra and experiencing that amount of snow and coldness. Although I couldn't handle the snow, it was nice to experience the city, and it gave me some answers to what I was looking for. That being an artist in Europe is possible because of the way they approached my work and the way they showed interest, this gave me the feeling that maybe Vienna was the right place. So we decided to try again, this time to come to Vienna around summertime, whichwas possible. It was when I arrived that I started getting rejections from the art world, because before, it had just been an introduction and visit. This time around I was staying a bit longer so I could see how to become an artist. When everything started going wrong—because almost all the spaces were replying, "We don't show African art, we don't show this type of art"—it was a big blow. For a moment I thought maybe what I was doing

was not good enough, then I turned around and asked why they asked me to participate the first time. This forced me to ask myself a lot of questions. That was 2013/14 for me.

EE   And then you enrolled at the Academy of Fine Arts Vienna?

AB   Yeah, the idea from there was: if I was not in the art circle, then I wouldn't know the right places to look for exhibitions. And because Vienna is also very white and everything is really exclusive, since I wasn't in the right space and didn't know the right people, I didn't know where to go. At that point my partner and I decided that I should enroll at the academy. I thought if that happened, maybe it would be possible to find one or two places to exhibit my works. The academy was also a place where a lot of things happened, there were a lot of possibilities. So I did enroll, and at the beginning I thought it was a waste of time. I had already studied in Ghana for four years, and now I was going to study for four years in Vienna. You know, I had people back home who depended on me to provide for them. So anytime I brought up the topic of me going back to school, people would urge me to find a job instead of continuing my studies. But the only thing— that was in Vienna—that I could do at the time was to either wash plates or clean, and I said to myself, I didn't come all the way here to be cleaning. No, that was not going to happen. So I stayed in the academy.

EE   You've said that when you were at the academy you learned how to be free to experiment and incorporate art-historical and conceptual aspects into your work.

AB   In Ghana, they told us what to do, and there was no room to stray. When I arrived in Vienna, we had space to experiment. So Vienna gave me the opportunity to practice freely. They didn't come and say, "This is how this bottle looks, and you have to paint it this way." If you didn't want to go to painting class, you didn't go. You could just stay in the studio and decide to do what you wanted to do. So that gave me the freedom of experimenting, which means that I stayed in my studio all the time. I already knew how to draw. I knew how to mix my colors; I knew how to paint. I knew how to stretch; I knew how to unstretch. So there were a lot of things that I didn't have to go learn because I already had that education. I think it gave me the upper hand to be able to just stay in the studio and experiment. That's what Vienna gave me.

EE   This is also where you were properly able to engage with the likes of Klimt and Schiele. Had you come across those artists before then?

AB   No, no. I mean, well, in Ghana you only get what you get. You don't really see much. I actually got to know all these artists when I arrived in Vienna. I didn't know who Klimt or Schiele or anybody was, but you see their stuff everywhere. Everywhere you go, it is there. So there were a lot of amazing and talented artists, but then there were always one or two or three or five people that always stood out. I had been thinking about what, how, and why they stood out from their peers. So I started looking into Klimt and playing around with my colors—or the surface or the texture itself—and that actually got me to look at Schiele's painting. When I looked at Schiele's painting, I was inspired by his use of color and integrated a similar color palette into my studio practice at the time.

EE   It's the colors. It's also Schiele's ability to think about the figure. These elegant, slim figures and these long fingers seemed to resonate with you in terms of what you're looking for, in terms of how to depict the body. Or were you already thinking along those lines anyway?

AB   Well, I wasn't really thinking much about the way he sketches or how his figures looked. I already knew the characters that I wanted to paint. I mean, at some point people were telling me

to stop painting Black people if I wanted to have a career, which I did for a while. But then I decided I wanted to have a career AND pick characters that I feel connected to. I feel comfortable painting non-Black people but emotionally, for me, it is not the same as painting Black faces, and so I painted a diversity of subjects for a while, and then I just went back to painting Black people. Like I said, I knew exactly what I wanted to paint. I just wanted to find a way to simplify it. I wanted to find a way to make it easy for people to remember. Similar to the way Schiele played with his composition, the colors, everything. It really was what I wanted to do with my work. But I had to find a way to do it so that it would become mine. I think that is what I've been able to do.

EE   Would your work have been the same if you'd studied in a different European city, if you haven't been in Vienna?

AB   I don't know. I mean, everything that happened, I can say was just coincidental, you know? It was not that I thought, "OK, I want to make this painting, and I want to do it with my finger." It wasn't like that at all. If I'm being honest, it was just that I had these friends who came by the studio and wanted me to be part of a music video by painting in it. At the time I was painting with brushes, since that was all I had studied. So I told myself that I was good with the brush and couldn't do anything wrong with the brush. But when they came, I didn't want to show them the process of making brushwork. So I did a quick sketch for them to be able to capture something. That is when I decided to just play with my finger. When they left, I was like, "This is cool."

EE   I guess you're looking for the visual language, and that takes time to evolve. It takes time for you to create that language. What's interesting to me is that you've got a very distinctive way of working, a very distinctive style. It seems to be based in this sense of depicting the Black figure with real complexity, with a physical thickness that comes from working with the finger, but then with the real delicacy, with real nuance. Each figure, each character feels like they have their own presence on the canvas.

AB   From the beginning I was thinking of making paintings. For me painting was a way of speaking. I think Vienna was a space where there was a language barrier, so I had to find replacements for the words that I wasn't able to find. I made paintings for that. It became less of a process of finding which characters I wanted to paint, and more about what exactly I want from them; how I want them to feel, what I want them to wear. Before it was more intuitive to a feeling. And so, I would say, before I was mostly painting for myself, but now I am painting for myself, but also for the majority that connects with my work.

EE   Do you have a sense of who the figures are in your paintings? You don't paint from life, do you?

AB   I used to. Once in a while, when I get a chance, I can sit people down and I paint from life. But most of the time I take pictures, or use pictures, and build the characters that I want.

EE   So that's the thing. Do you have those characters in your head? Are you looking at the picture and saying, OK, look, this can be something, or are you building it up? Do you have an end point in mind from the beginning?

AB   It is energy. I'm looking for people that I know that fit into that energy. I might see a picture of someone, and I like the pose, that is an inspiration. Now from the pose that I take, I will have to find a character that I want to create that has the energy that I'm looking for. The pose is an inspiration.

EE   Color seems so important in the work: the blues, the pinks, the yellows, the greens … What role does it play for you?

AB   You know the way you feel and the ways you choose to express yourself. For me, color is the way I feel. I like to think that even if I'm going through difficulties, I think of myself as some-thing bright. I had a semester where I was only experimenting with the color yellow because it was so cold and gray, I needed some sun. Where I come from you have sun all year round, so I'm not going to allow a couple of months to just give me grays. I decided this whole semester is gray, but I am going to imagine myself in Accra, where it is sunny, and I'm just going to be yellow. That's how it started.

EE   To what extent are the figures and the characters you paint based on you?

AB   When I arrived in Vienna and was rejected, I actually started painting myself a bit more because I felt that if I don't know myself that well, then I can't offer much to others. I think in every show that I have done there's always a self-portrait. For me, when I think of other characters, I think, "This could be me." But I mean it's not all the time that you find yourself in that situation or in that space, but it could be me. When I think of people that I want to paint, I think of people not necessarily who have a similar energy, but I think of people that do the things that I would want to do, or I'd like to see happening. I think of characters that generally just have a lively and welcoming presence. People who control or command spaces naturally have power in the way they pose, and that's what I'd like to be able to emulate with the figures in my work. I want my presence to be felt, and that is exactly what I managed to do with the characters that I paint, to be able for them to command the spaces they inhabit.

EE   Yeah, I'm thinking of the painting *Green Beret* (fig. 1), for instance, one of your best-known paintings in that we've seen it take a number of different forms.

AB   I think sometimes when I take a picture, or when I have an inspiration for my picture, I also allow the picture to direct me to where it's supposed to go. Sometimes you have an idea, but it's not all the time that your idea is good, and so you have to be open enough to see which direction that inspiration is willing to take you. I had thought about the color palette for *Green Beret* already, but sometimes when you are in the studio it just happens and then I just flow with it.

EE   Let's talk about self-portraits. Like you say, self-portraits are a recurring aspect of your exhibitions. I'm interested in the choices you make in terms of how you depict yourself. Why, for instance, some of the naked self-portraits? What's the decision-making there?

AB   Those were bodies of work I did over time. While I was in Vienna from 2014 to 2017, I often experienced hyper sexualization and I wanted to find a way to deal with it. Where I come from there's nothing wrong with enjoying sex, and I didn't want to think that now that I was in Vienna, people were only sexualizing the Black body. I used nudity as a tool and starting point toward illustrating a more accurate and holistic depiction of Black people. So I started with myself as nude, because they know the Black body … and then I decided, I want to add intellect to the work. The Black body is intellectual. The Black body has had a lot of positive historical and social impact. I wanted to start from what people know, and add aspects of humanity, joy, and intellectualism that they decide to disregard. I don't want to use my body in the space, I am only using myself as the subject to complain about the fact that audiences in Vienna didn't want to see accurate depictions of Black life. So I wanted to show them an expanded visual understanding of what Blackness and Black figures could look like outside of their limited beliefs.

EE   There's also the series of self-portraits with books: *Black Skin, White Masks* by Frantz Fanon (p. 133), *Ghana Must Go* by Taiye Selasi (p. 135), and *Shadow of Imana* by Véronique Tadjo (fig. 2).

AB   When I did those works, I wanted to find a way to deal with how people were looking at me and what they thought of me. I know a lot of people have been doing work about Black bodies and stereotyping. I didn't want to do work that complained, I wanted to do work that suggested how I wanted to be seen. I understand the box given to me, but I also want people to know that I am much bigger than the box assigned. So, I decided to add these references of Black intellectuality with the nude Black body, because that is what they refused to acknowledge. That was the starting point for me.

EE   Yeah. The Belvedere show is your largest exhibition to date. Do you know how many works are in the show?

AB   We are expecting more than fifty paintings. I am currently in conversation with collectors that I know have my paintings

in Europe, or specifically in Vienna, to contribute some paintings that have not been seen for a very long time.

EE   What's the experience like of looking back at these works and being reunited with them?

AB   I usually don't think of it that much. But you know from time to time when I think of Vienna, I realize I lived there for six years, and it was the space where everything started for me. In terms of my career, in terms of experimenting and thinking of painting more, and testing surfaces and textures. Thinking about the title for the show, love brought me to Vienna, but I don't think my staying in Vienna had anything to do with love. It was more of wanting to prove that I have something good to offer. It was more for me to prove that maybe what they were saying about what I had to do to have a successful career was wrong. Going back and exhibiting the work at the Belvedere, which are all Black individuals. I don't think that has anything to do with love, but I'm still feeling the love that brought me to Vienna, which has allowed me to be the artist I am today.

EE   What's the feeling then that you come to with this show? Is it showing "them" or is it proving something to yourself? Is it simply asserting here you are?

AB   Oh, I think I can already take out the notion of proving, because I have nothing to prove. I think the Belvedere show is for the people who are in Vienna, most importantly the Black and brown people who are in Vienna. This show is for them to feel comfortable and seen. It's for them to go into that space and feel like they are included and part of the space. Because most of the time when you go to the Belvedere—and in Vienna in general—you only see white people. I think when you go to see

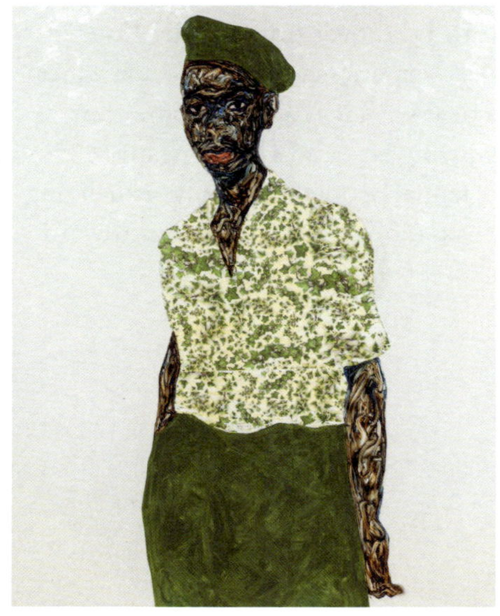

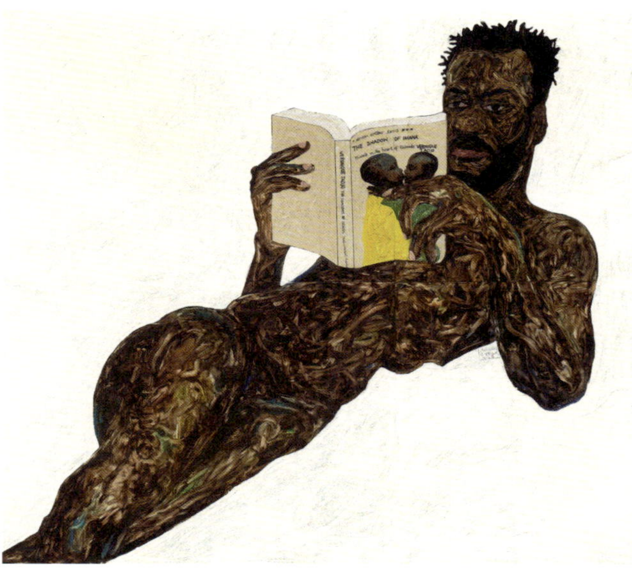

Fig. 1
Amoako Boafo, *Green Beret*, 2020

Fig. 2
Amoako Boafo, *Shadow of Imana*, 2018

this show, even if you are the only Black person in the space, there are a lot of Black characters in the paintings, so you feel like the space is yours. It is not for me to prove anything to the Viennese. Absolutely not It's just to make the people feel welcomed as if they are not the only people there. I mean, of course the paintings are not talking, but they are talking.

EE   Yes, they're speaking. James Baldwin talked about the experience of being a Black person in Europe specifically, where you are often cast as an outsider, as a stranger.

AB   I want them to feel like they belong in the space.

EE   Yeah, that's the thing. And also, within the exhibition, visitors will see your works next to Schiele, next to Klimt. Is that important for you?

AB   Yes, for me it's important. I would like to see my paintings next to them, just to see how people will interact and how they will engage with the paintings. I also want people to see that although there are similarities, they are completely different. I think if that is done, then I can have my name, not Schiele, but Amoako. You know it's alright to have people think about painting and think of great artists, but I also just want to maintain my name. You don't have to think of my painting and always think about Klimt and Schiele.

EE   You talk about celebrating Blackness. What does Blackness look like or feel like for you?

AB   Blackness is pleasure. Blackness is luxury. For me, Blackness is everything. I don't know what you cannot get from Blackness. And that is why it's a little bit confusing when people look and think of all the negative things associated with Blackness. Again, that is what they want to think. But I have my view. Blackness is luxury.

EE   I wonder what the energy will feel like to have so many works in the same space.

AB   I think I am going to be experiencing it for the first time as everyone else will be doing. There are some paintings that I have not seen for a while, for a very long time. And there are paintings that were the beginning of how I started with making my finger painting and how it has transformed. I also want to see them hanging, just to see how I have improved over the years. So I'm excited about it. You know, it's not all the time that you get to see all your paintings in one space, after years of making paintings. Yes, there's the body of work that you put together and then you do a show, which will be from, let's say, 2022 to 2023. But then this one is from, I don't know, from 2016, to 2024. So I'm looking forward to enjoying the span of work that I've done over the years.

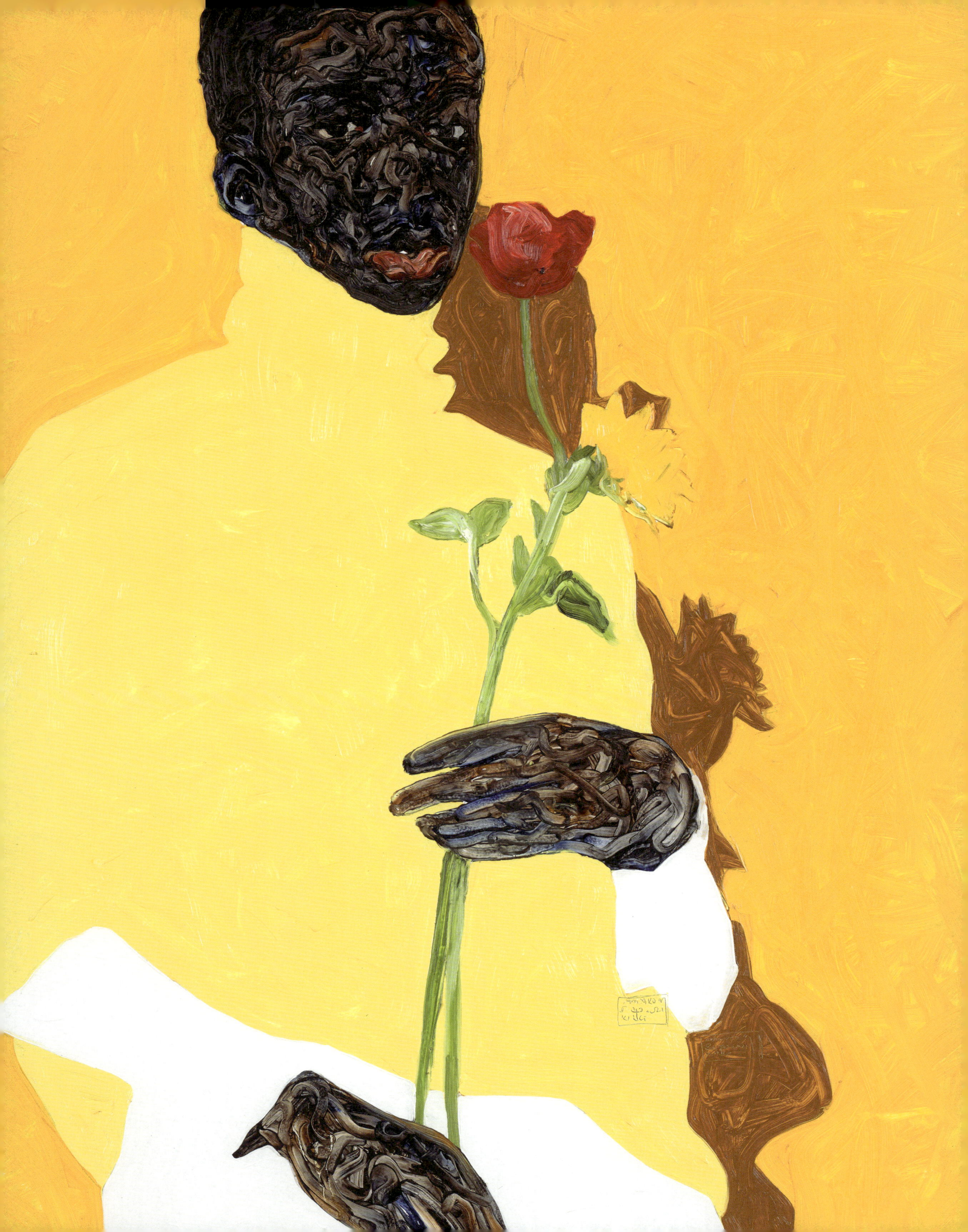

The Vienna Succession

Taiye Selasi

In 1916 the Liljevalchs Konsthall—today one of Sweden's most famous galleries—opened on an island called Djurgården in Stockholm. The building was designed by Swedish architect Carl Bergsten; having won a scholarship to study in Vienna, Bergsten was greatly inspired by Austrian titan Otto Wagner. Perhaps unsurprisingly, then, one of the gallery's first exhibitions was dedicated entirely to Austrian art. On August 15, 1917, with a world war ravaging Europe, an eclectic group of artists made their Scandinavian debut: from Vienna Secessionists (Anton Hanak, Gustav Klimt) to Neukunstgruppe Secessionists (Egon Schiele) to Expressionists (Anton Faistauer, Oskar Kokoschka) and beyond: lesser-known handicraft artisans, and designers of Austrian haute couture. At the helm of this motley crew was German-Moravian architect Josef Hoffmann, so committed to presenting a wholly new vision of Austria that he would abandon his decade-old views on curation. As art critic Elizabeth Clegg writes, Hoffmann "eschewed his former preference for centring an entire display on one or two stars (Klimt in Paris in 1900, Klimt and the German-Bohemian sculptor Franz Metzner in Vienna in 1908)" and did so in order to offer a particular account of 'Austria'" to an eager Swedish public.[1] If the show had no definitive focal point—no single artist, no single region, no single medium—it nevertheless offered a clear definition of Austrian art: hybrid, grounded, unpreoccupied by the past, inherently fascinated by the future. For Erwin Hanslik, the geographer who served as its "ideological spokesman," the exhibition was to be viewed in its conspicuous diversity as an expression of Austria itself: "a harmoniously multi-ethnic whole threatened by [...] separatist nationalism but truly a model for the peaceful future of humanity."

Now I know what you're thinking. What does a group show of Austrian art in Sweden in 1917 have to do with the solo show of a Ghanaian artist in Austria in 2024? For a start, there is the matter of youth. Now forty years old, Amoako Boafo did not receive any formal art education until the age of twenty. That, just two short decades later, he has catapulted himself from the halls of a West African vocational school onto the walls of the Belvedere is almost unbelievable. That it is not also *unprecedented* speaks to the contemporary phenomenon that Boafo exemplifies: the emergence of astonishingly talented, staggeringly young artists that have been termed Africa's New Creative Wave.

Think: Ghanaian-British Lynette Yiadom-Boakye, shortlisted for the Turner Prize at age thirty-six; Ethiopian-American Julie Mehretu, who received an astounding five-million-dollar commission at age thirty-seven; Nigerian-American Kehinde Wiley, selected to paint an American presidential portrait at age forty. I reference Boafo's peers not to diminish his own singular and spectacular achievement but rather, in contextualizing it, to dismiss the notion that we should be shocked, in the age of luminary African art, to find a luminary African artist at a preeminent museum. If we do find Boafo's presence at the Belvedere (and in the Upper Museum no less) jarring, we might find it interesting to ask ourselves why. It is not that the artist is African, I have heard some say; it is that he is young. But this, too, I dismiss. Certainly, in any other European capital, one might expect some equivocation about exhibiting an artist so young at an institution so hallowed. But Austria, as the 1917 exhibition *Österrikiska utställningen* reminds us, has always embraced youth as central to its national creative character. At fifty-five, Klimt was that show's most famous artist but by no means its most dominant. As curator, Hoffmann responded to the mandate to represent Austria by explicitly foregrounding younger Austrians too. Writes Clegg: "While an effective merging of generational identities had occurred in 1912, when the (older) Klimtgruppe and the (younger) Neukunstgruppe had joined forces, […] the 1917 show was the first state-sponsored Austrian venture […] in which older and younger artists participated on the same terms." She goes on, "In Stockholm, […] no fewer than five other exhibitors were each allotted an entire room, all but one of them still classifiable as 'young'. The eastern Tyrolean Albin Egger-Lienz and the Salzburg sophisticate Anton Faistauer were given the two large central spaces […] and were expressly so positioned in order to draw attention, through provocative contrasts, to the thematic and stylistic diversity found within contemporary Austrian art." If Hoffmann had it right, a refusal to balkanize artists on the basis of age rests at the core of the modern artistic identity of Austria. Then, there is nothing particularly radical but rather something fundamentally *Austrian* in the choice to exhibit the works of forty-year-old Boafo alongside pieces from 140 years before.

The same might be said—that there is something of Austria—in Boafo's art itself, but not in the context of the familiar and often facile question of "influences." It is true that Boafo (like the aforementioned Bergsten) won a scholarship to study in Vienna, and it is truly remarkable *how*. If I was unsurprised to learn that, as a child in Accra, Boafo was unusually gifted in drawing, I was startled to discover that he originally intended to make his name in tennis. It was only as his sports dreams began to fade and his single mum began to fret that he enrolled in the Ghanatta College of Art and Design. Here, at the same "crafts school" (Boafo's words) that trained rising star Annan Affotey, Boafo learned the nuts and bolts of painting. In the years that followed he began painting portraits, working as a pallbearer to earn money for art supplies. Then, completely by chance, he crossed paths with an artist from Vienna. This young Austrian painter, in Ghana doing charity work, had taken to creating murals on the walls of rural schools. Boafo met the painter through mutual friends and learned of Austrian scholarship opportunities through the painter. In 2014, after two short stays in Vienna, Boafo enrolled at the city's Academy of Fine Arts.

Now, again, I know what you're thinking. Or rather, I know what we've been conditioned to think comes next. When artists with magnificent abilities but mediocre educations leave the South for further study in the North, we are taught to imagine these artists as raw, somehow unformed, on their arrival in Europe. In a naturally talented Ghanaian painter trained at a college in urban Accra, we are told to look for the *seeds* of artistic potential and not for an artist. But Boafo is clear: he did not come to Vienna to become a painter. He was *already* a portraitist when he arrived, one who knew just what he lacked (a more refined technique) and just what he sought (a more singular personal style). Boafo began his Austrian education as a student of contemporary African portraitists such as Yiadom-Boakye and Wiley, and of American stalwarts such as Kerry James Marshall and Henry Taylor. Admiring Yiadom-Boayke's simplicity, for instance, he asked himself how he might declutter his own compositions. Marveling at Toyin Ojih Odutola's pen strokes, he asked what kind of brushwork he might use to achieve that kind of detail. Drawn to Marshall's chiaroscuro, he vowed to learn to render dark figures that radiate light. And he did. Tempting as it can be to search the Austrian painting canon for Boafo's influences, the artist's primary references would seem to look more like him. It is not, he says, that studying European portraitists under Austrian professors did not improve his technique. It did. "But Austrians always question blackness. For them my figures were always too dark. The question was always, Can you brighten them a little?" He laughs. "They said that if I wanted to have a career in painting then I should paint white people."

The irony. Perhaps the most conspicuous effects of Boafo's Austrian education can be seen in the care with which he treats his subjects. "I discovered that I do not command any space in Vienna," he says. "I want my subjects to control their spaces." In formal study Boafo found both the time and the tools to develop what he calls his own handwriting, a singular approach to portraiture as instantly recognizable as his heroes, and unwavering (some critics call it repetitive). But it was formal study *in Vienna* that clarified the story that he wanted to tell with that writing: the story, the infinite stories, of black selfhood and self-possession. If we are eager to identify Austrian influences in Boafo's art, we might begin by imagining the artist's daily life in Austria; by inquiring about the various erasures that he has endured in Vienna, both at the academy and in the city at large; by recognizing that the brown faces and bodies so lovingly, even languidly, rendered in his portraits claim a space so often denied to their portraitist. Boafo speaks of this denial both openly and calmly, as one fully at peace. But not passive. In 2017 he opened an arts space, called WE DEY x space, to support, he says, "black and brown artists who feel invisible in Vienna." WE DEY x space's stated mission: "To change the uneven power structure within the Viennese art scene by creating a self-organised art space in which BPoC artists can show their work in a self-determined way."

It will not shock us, of course, to learn that Boafo and his community of non-white artists have faced discrimination in Austria. (According to one report, 1,300 incidents of racism occurred in the country last year alone.) But it might offer us pause. What of the Austria, the vision of Austria, that "harmoniously multi-ethnic whole," exhibited over a century ago in Stockholm? In 1917, just as in 2024, the world was being torn limb from limb by the bloodiest kinds of conflict. And still, against that backdrop of virulent extremism and violent nationalism, a hopeful vision of Austria emerged. German-Silesian Hanslik and German-Moravian Hoffmann (neither man born an Austrian) imagined a national creative identity animated by youth, enriched by multiplicity, and expanded by international interaction. What vision of Austria, and of Austrian art, succeeded theirs? What is, has been, or will be the "Vienna Succession"? I cannot say. But I would like to believe that we might trace a line from *their* show, their Austria, and its future-facing ideological legacy to the future expressed in *this* show; that we might look upon the works of Amoako Boafo, not born an Austrian either, and ask: what could be a more natural home for the work of this naturally gifted artist than *this* country?

1 All quotes from Elizabeth Clegg, "War and Peace at the Stockholm 'Austrian Art Exhibition of 1917,'" *Burlington Magazine*, yr. 154, no. 1315 (October 2012), pp. 676–88.

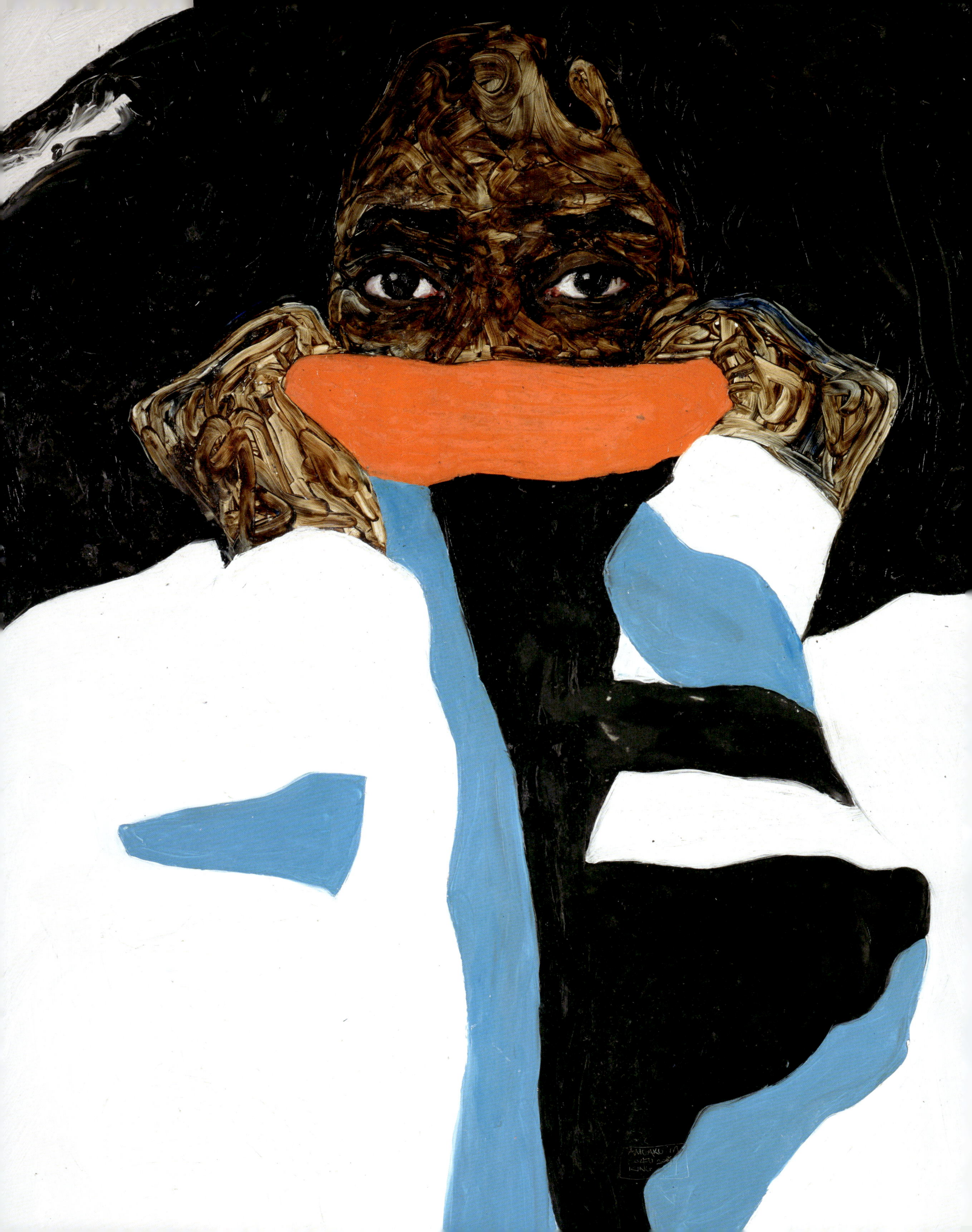

Answering Gaze

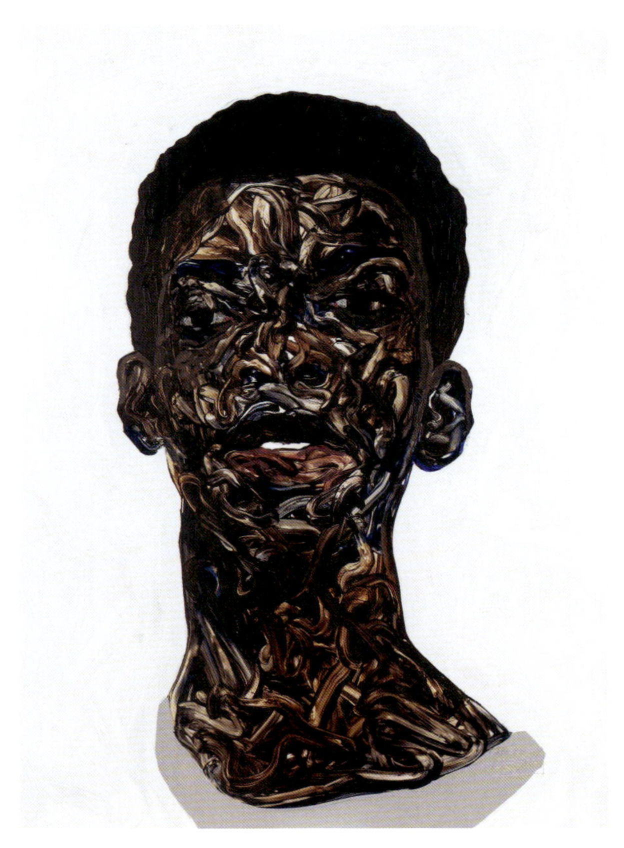

Grey Collar

2022

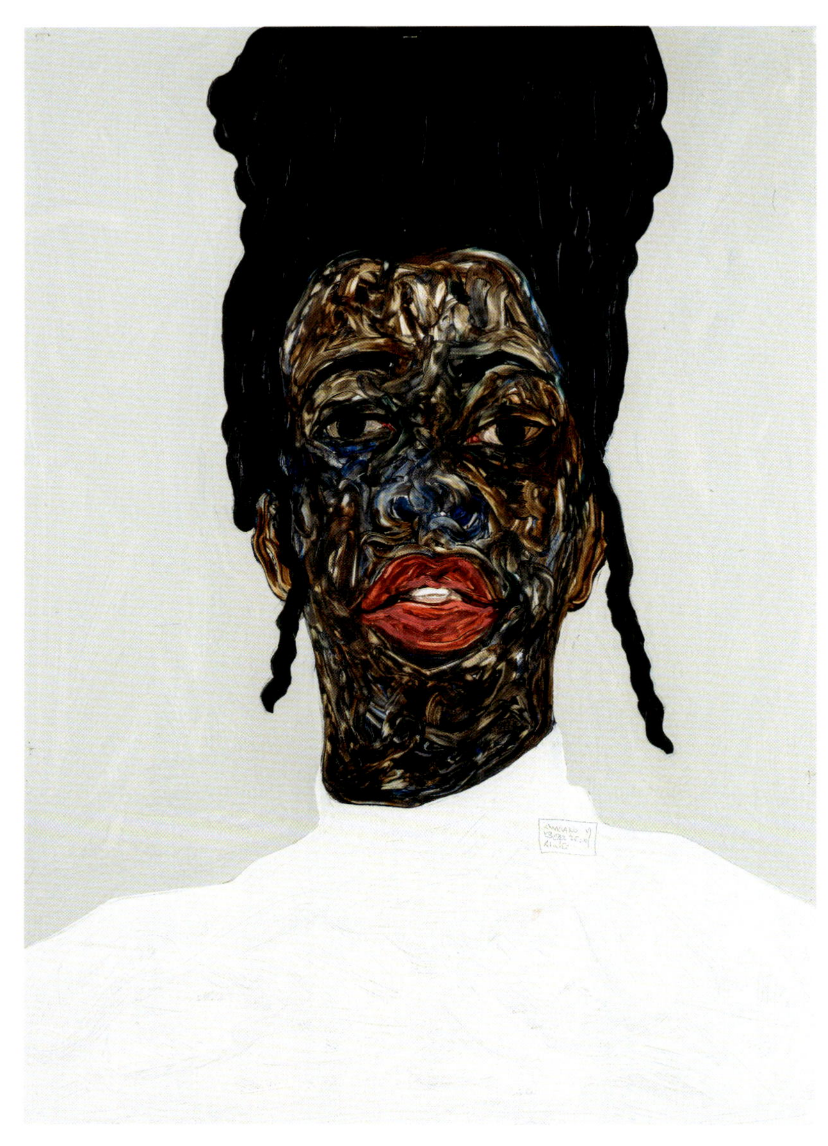

Chinese Collar
2021

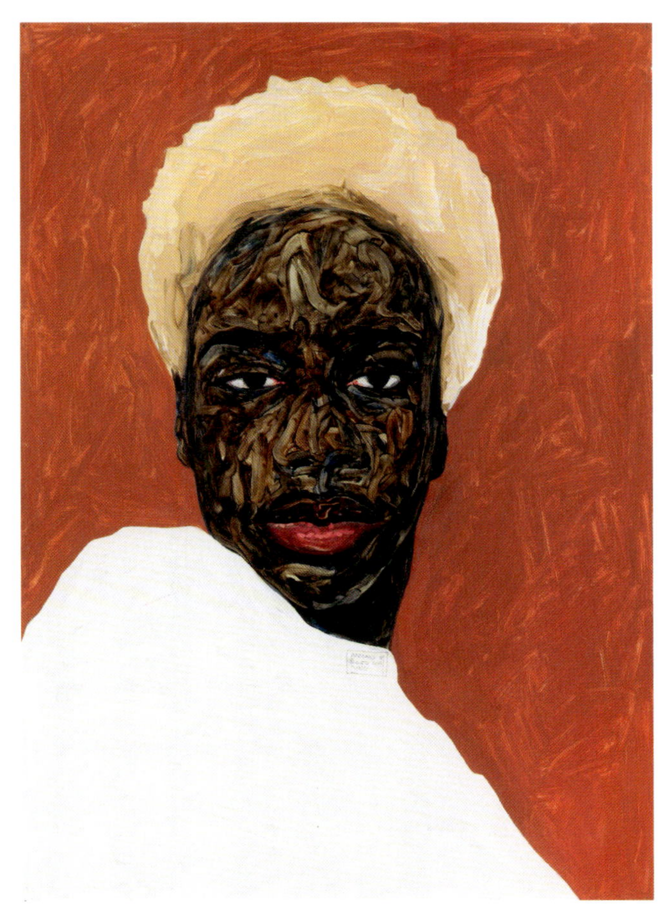

Blondie

2019

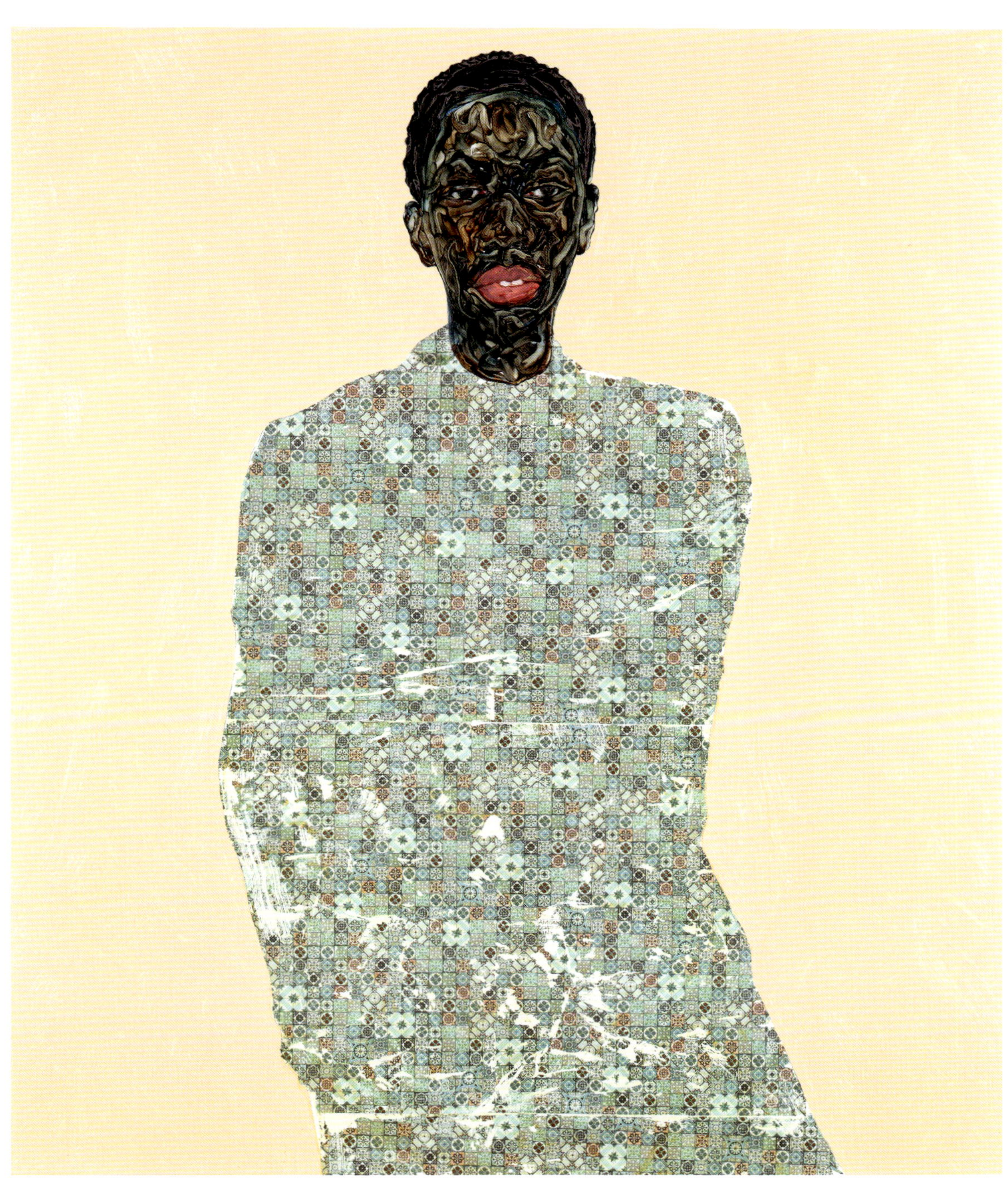

Cobinnah
2019

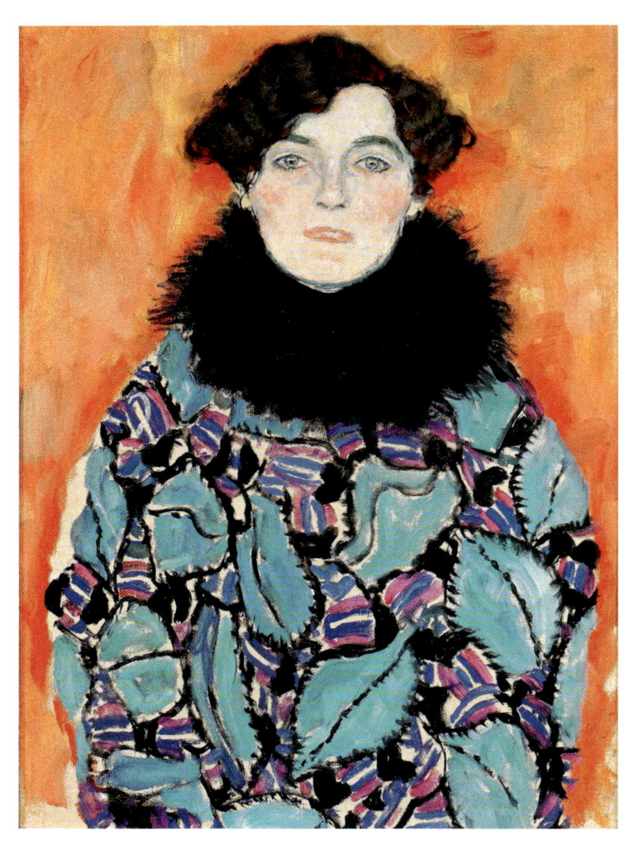

Gustav Klimt

Johanna Staude
1917/18

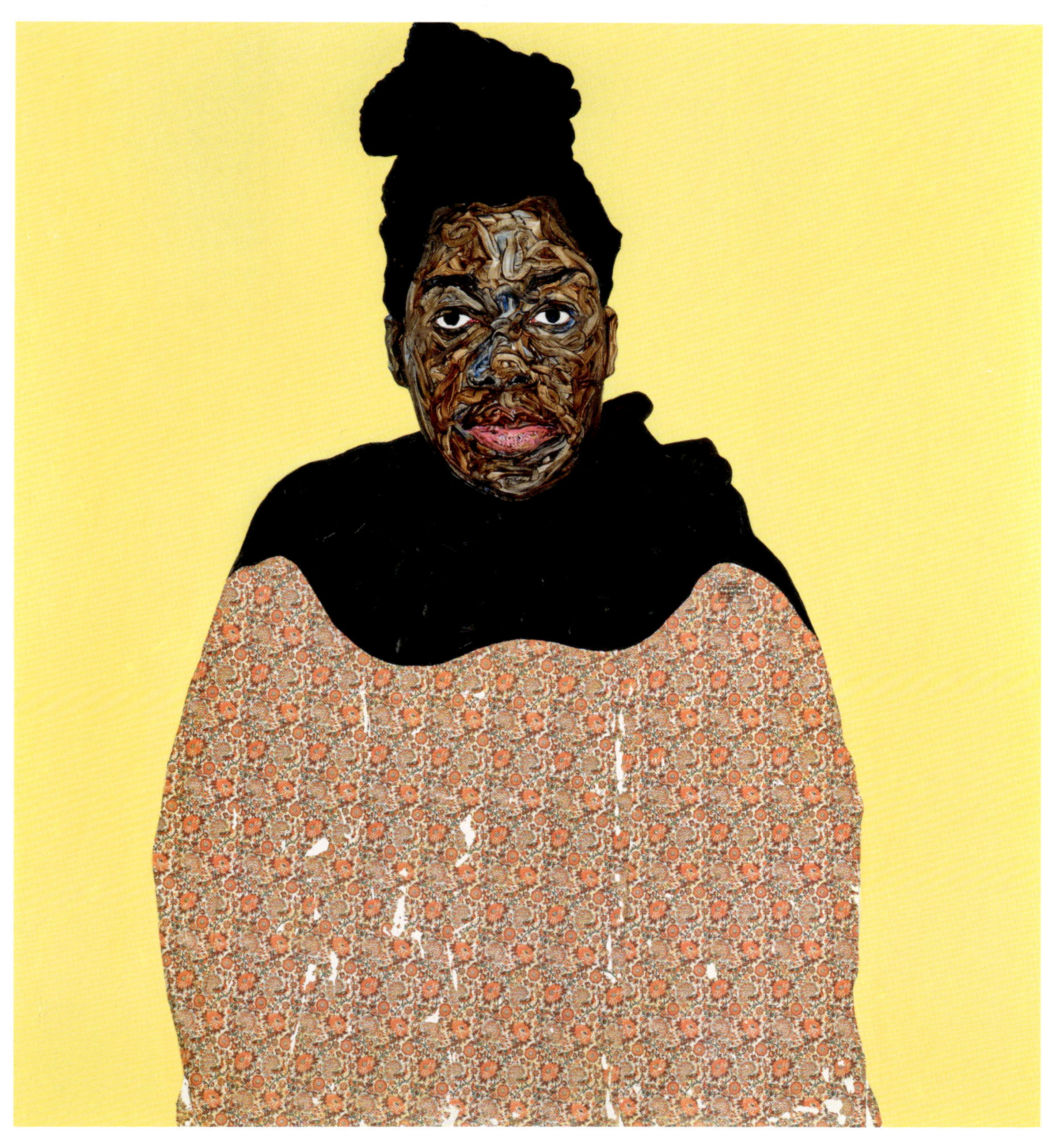

Enyonam's Black Shawl
2020

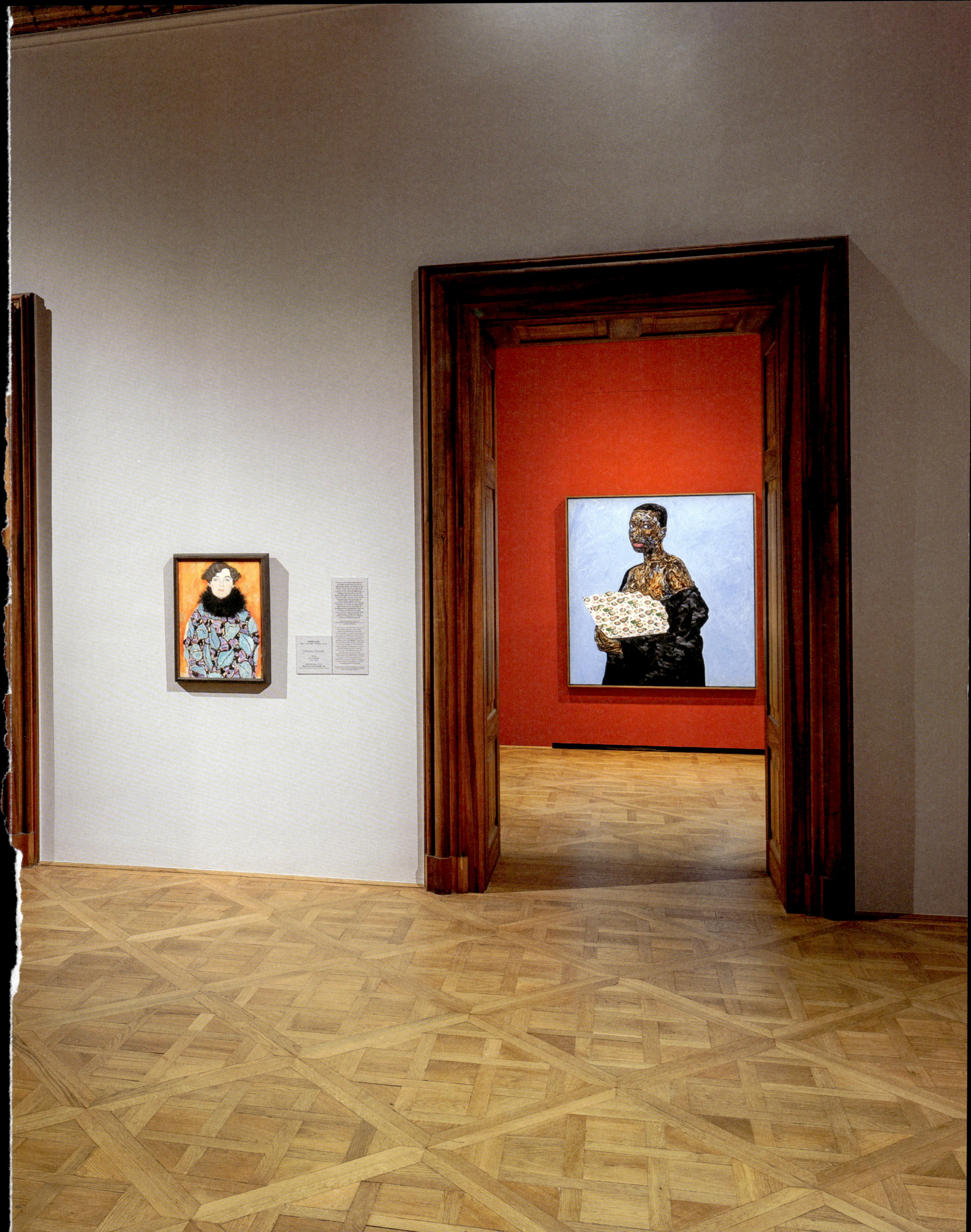

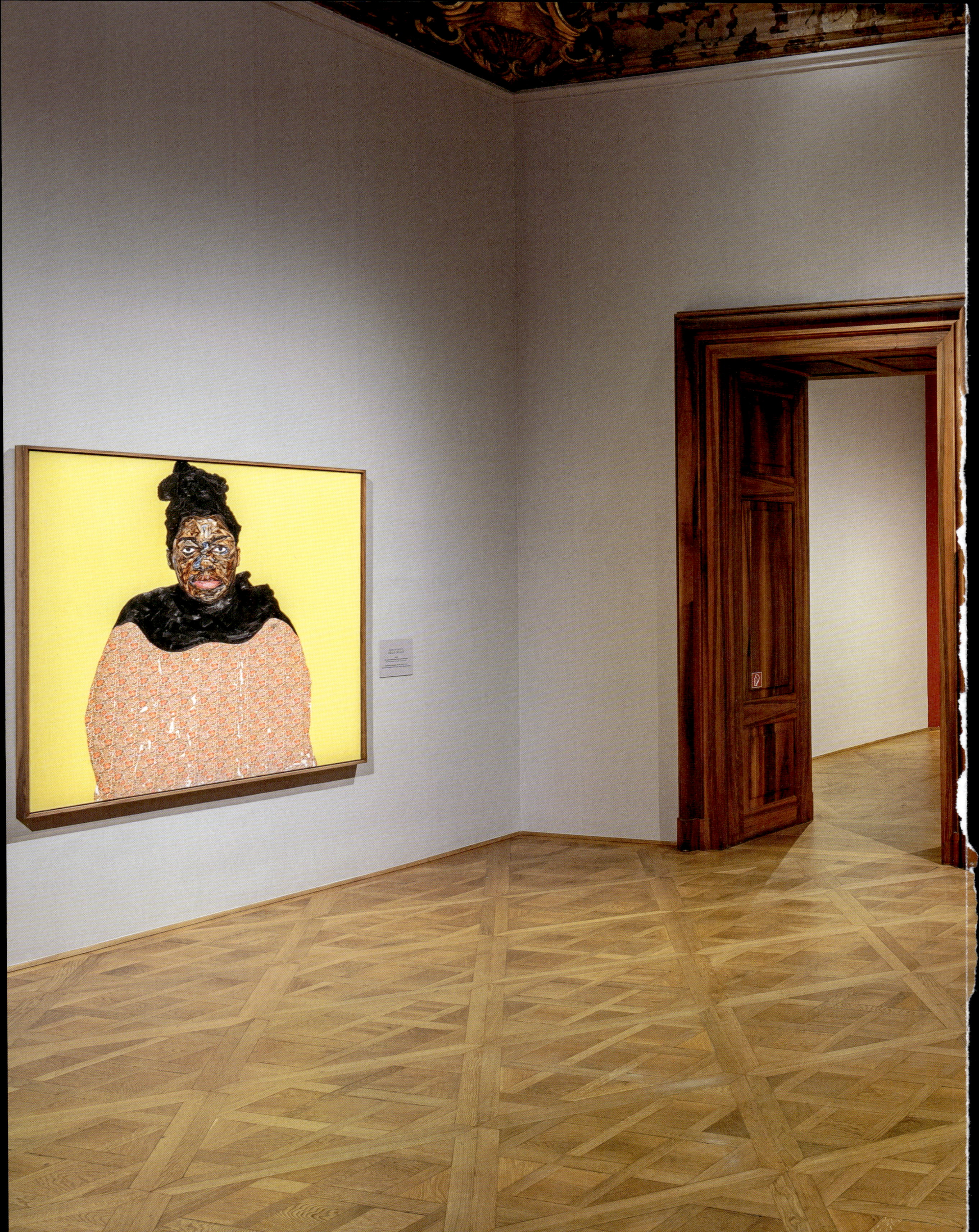

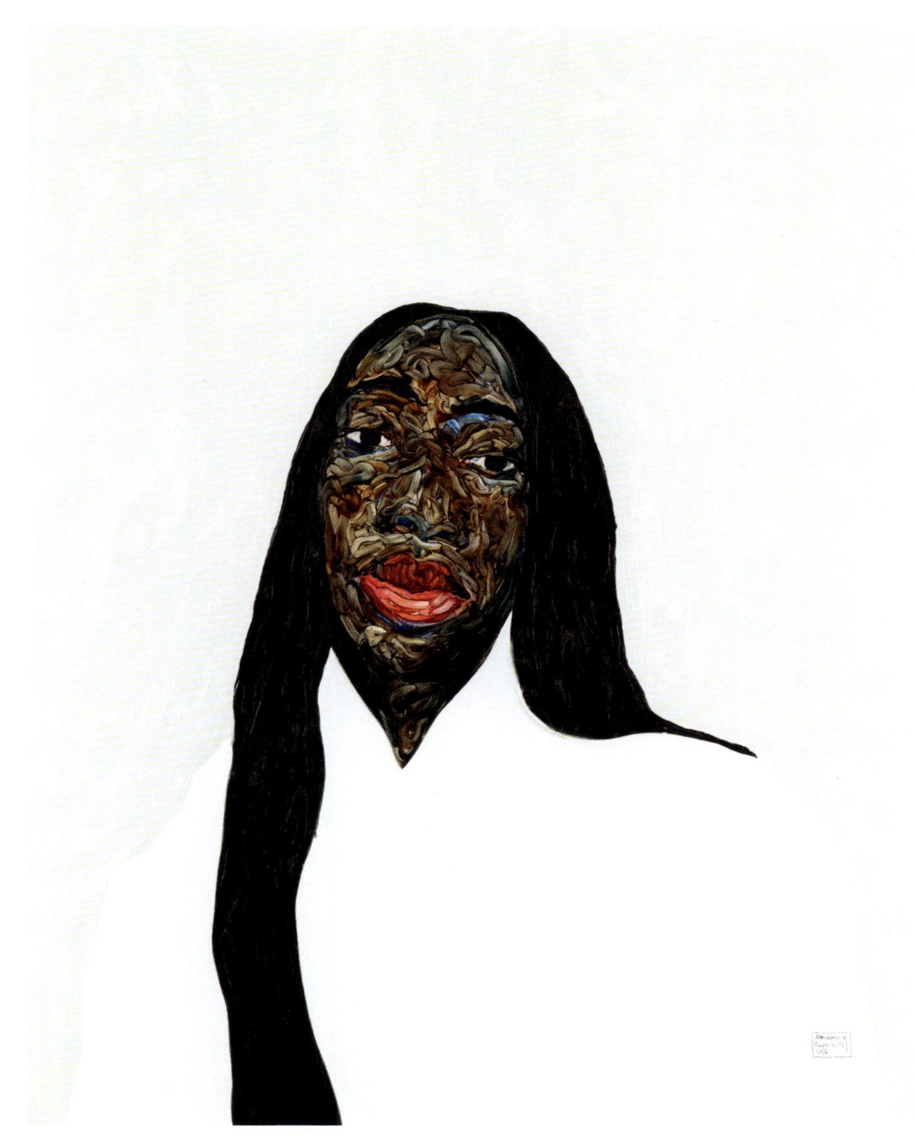

Owusu
2019

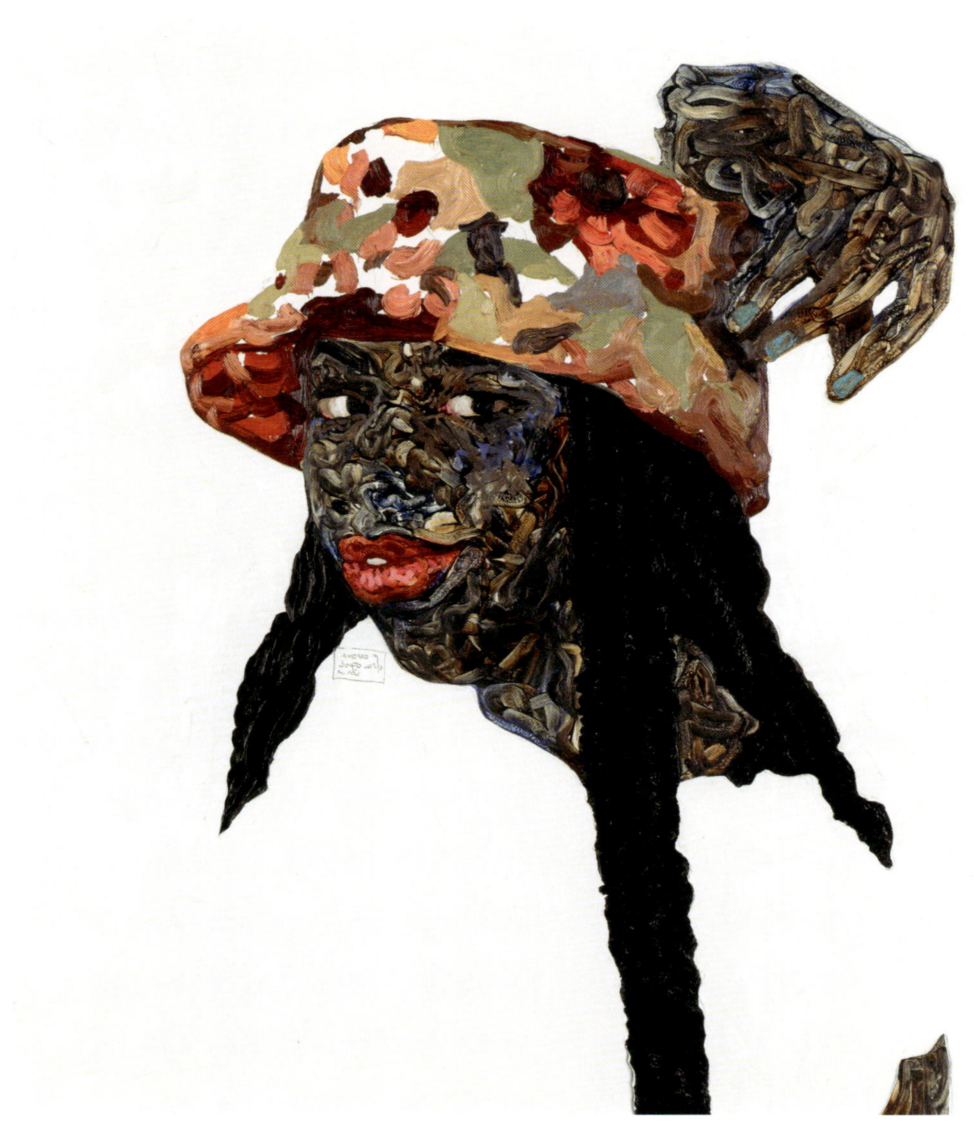

Multicolored Bucket Hat
2023

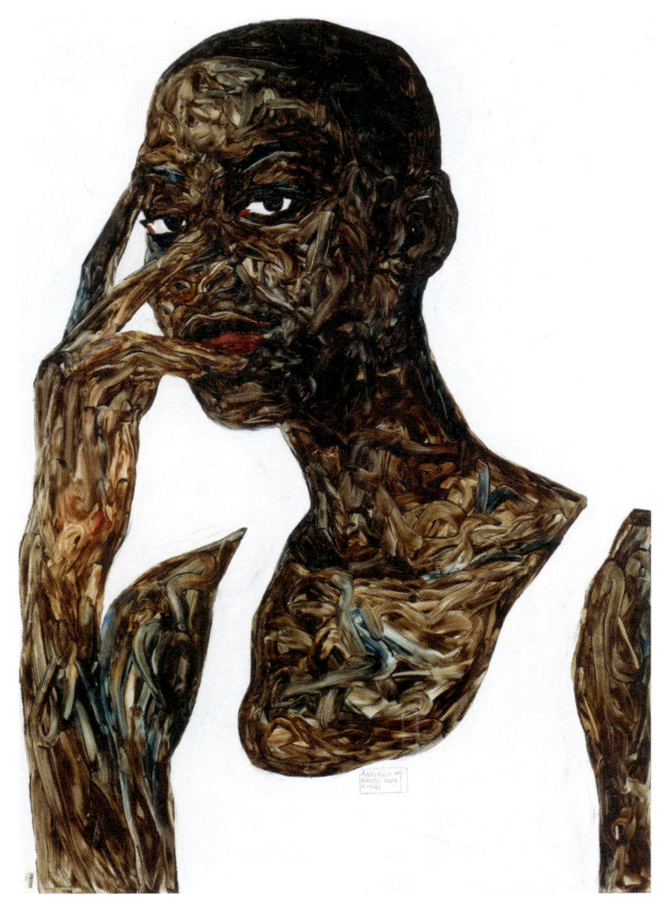

Looking Through Two Fingers
2018

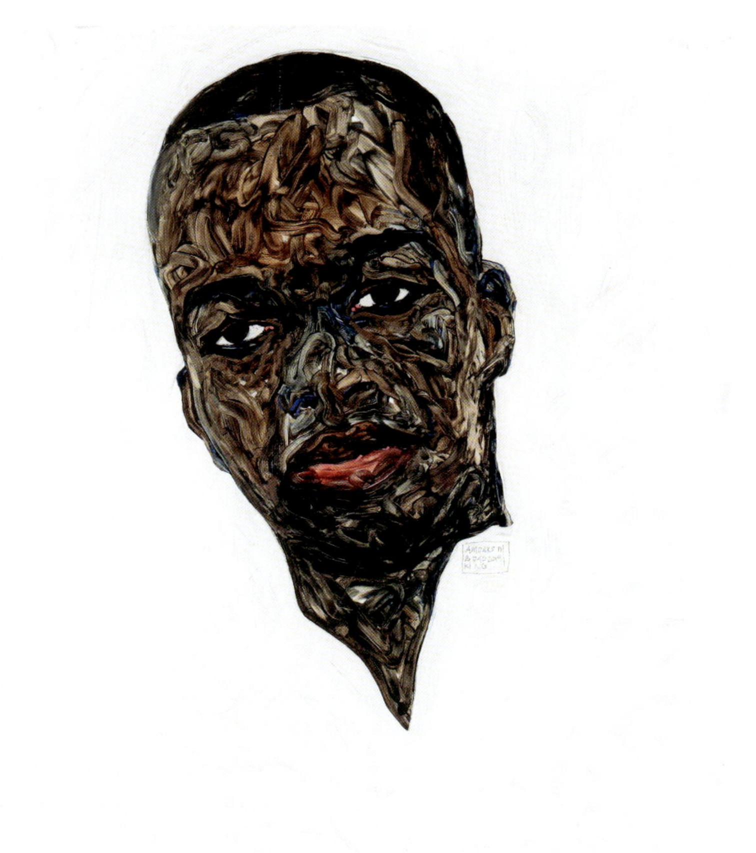

Jona
2019

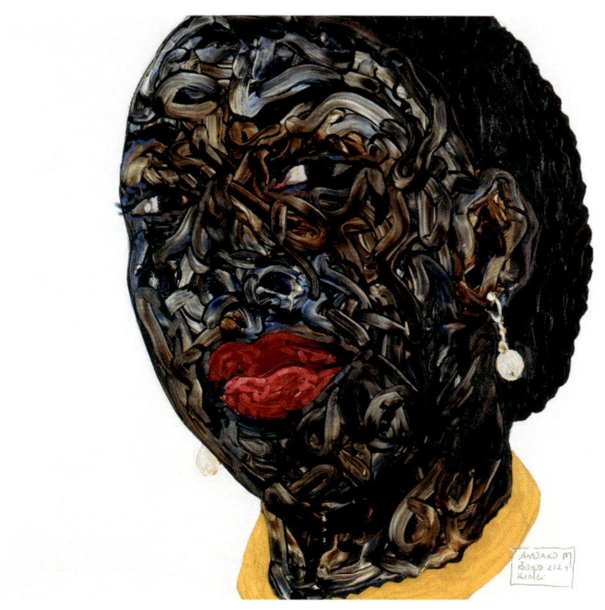

Phase I—Ayana

2024

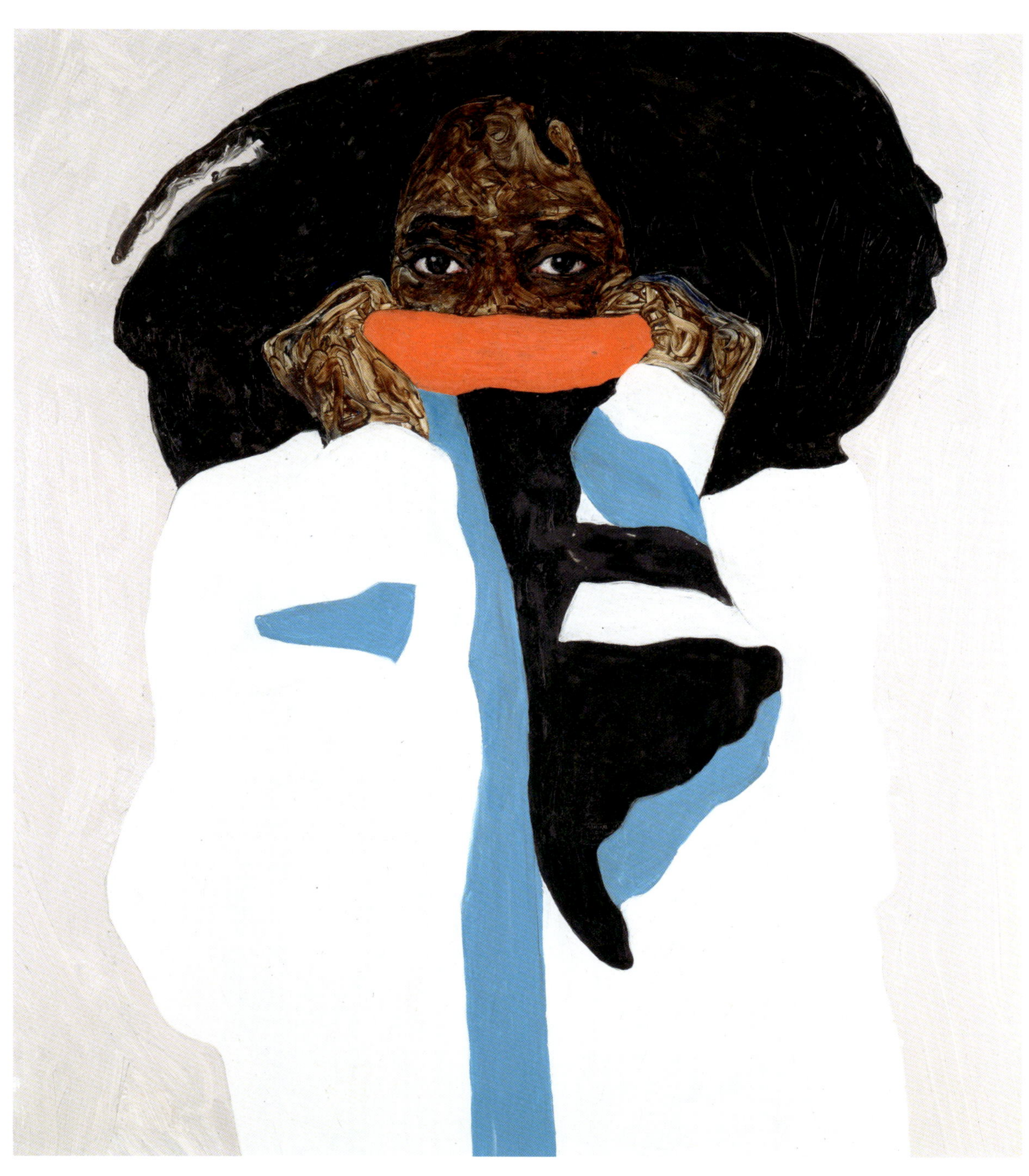

Orange, Black, Baby Blue, and White
2018

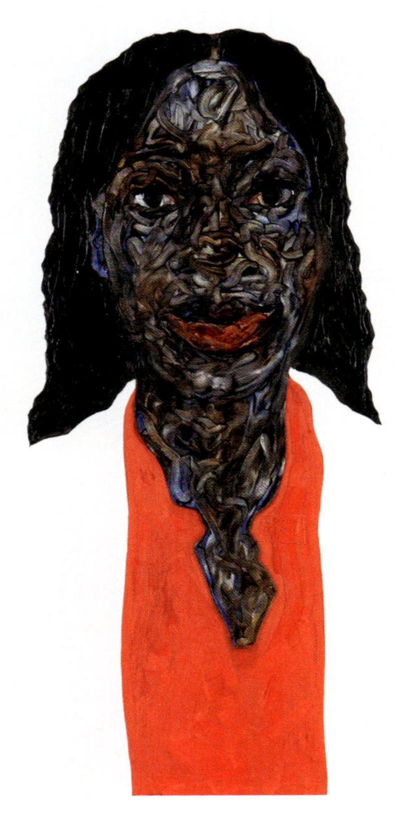

Red Undershirt

2022

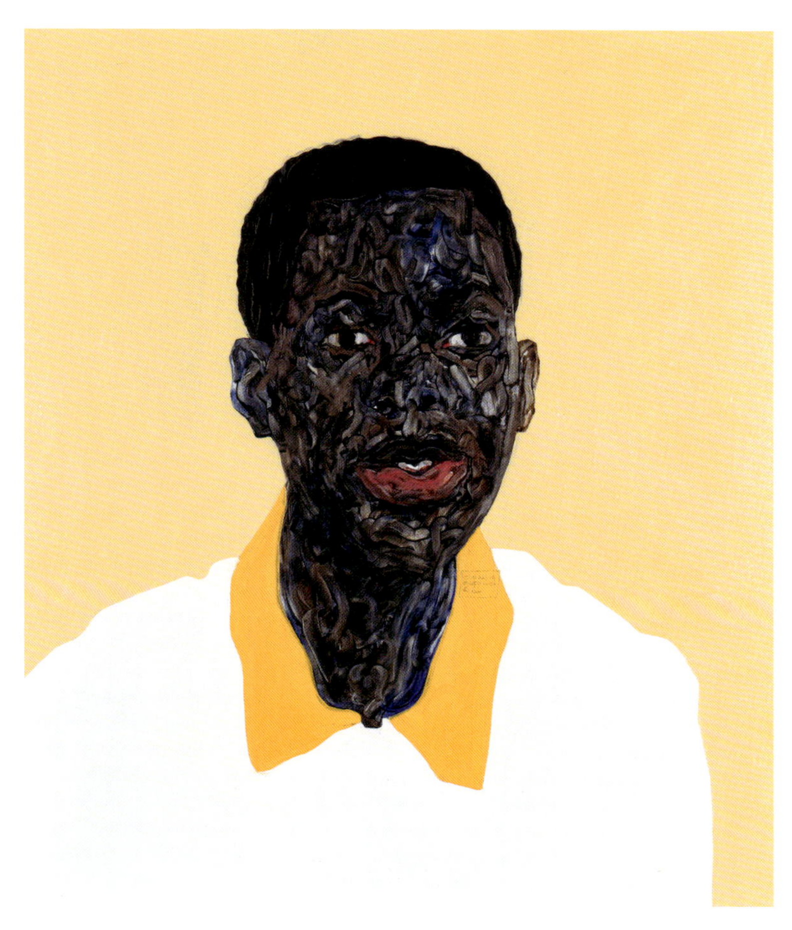

Yellow Collar

2022

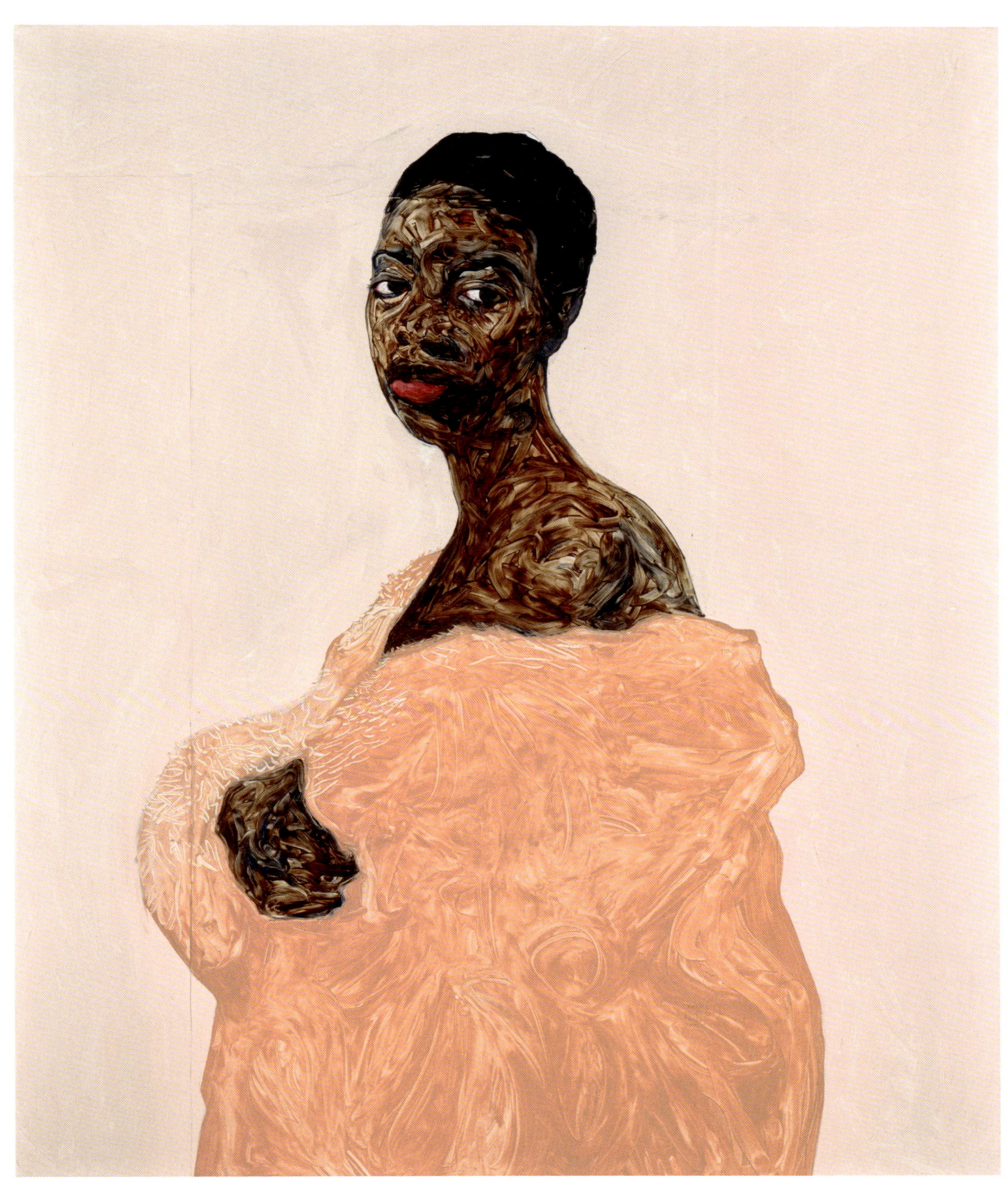

Untitled
2018

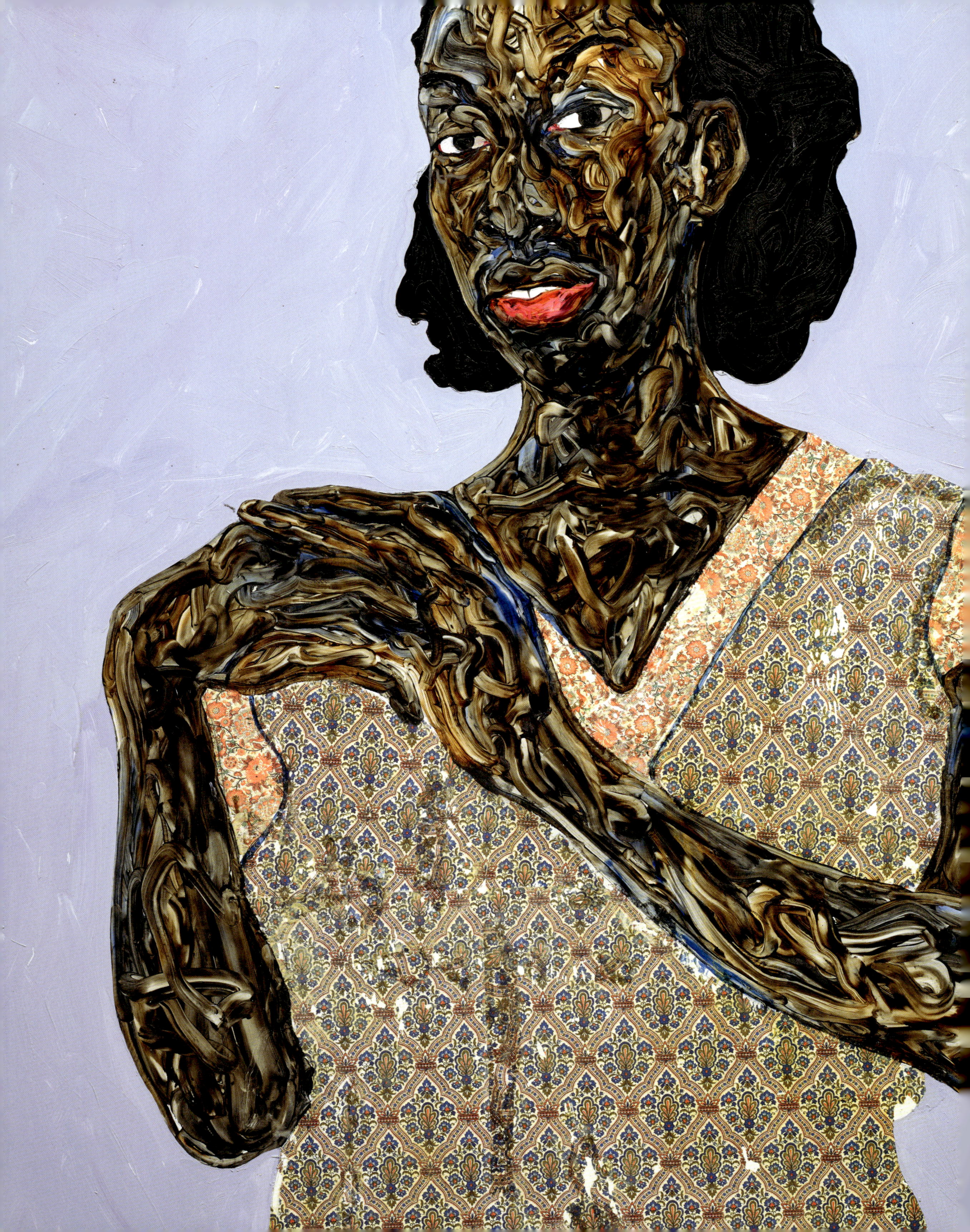

Viennese Women

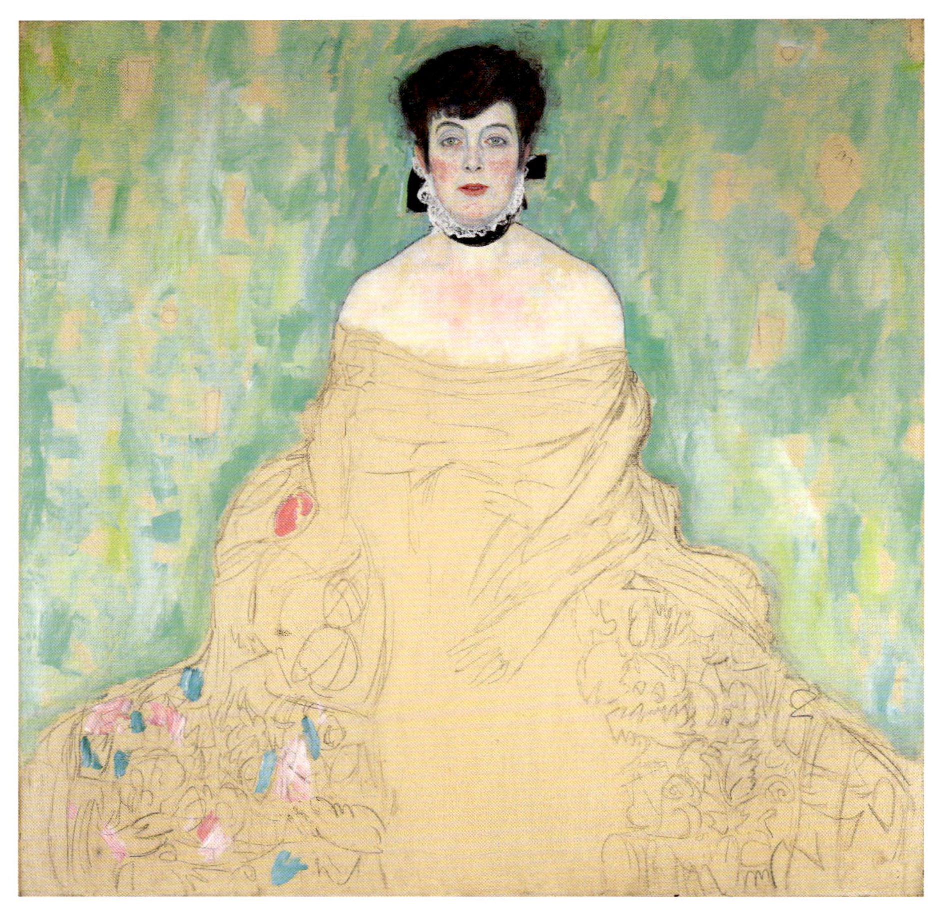

Gustav Klimt

Amalie Zuckerkandl
1917/18

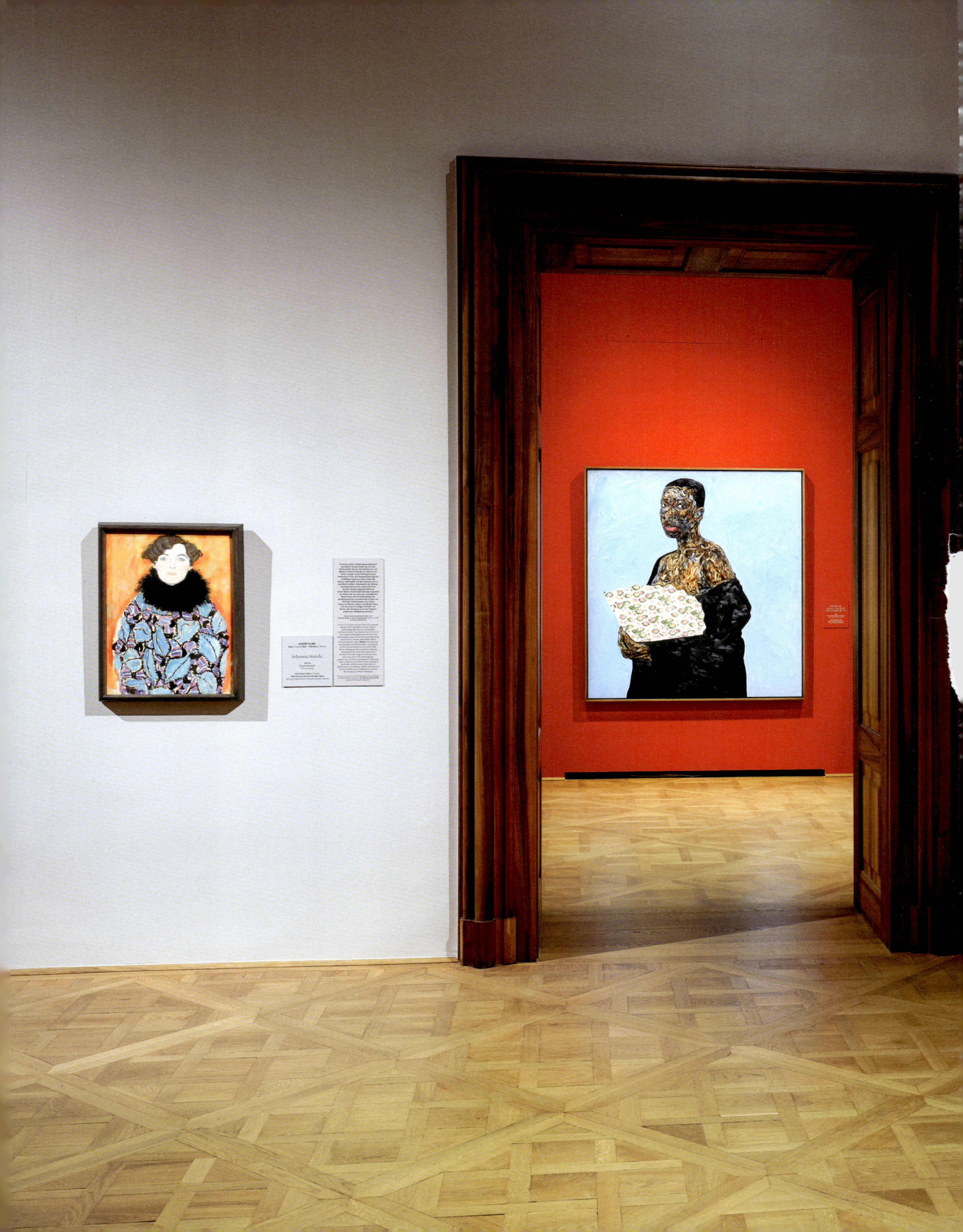

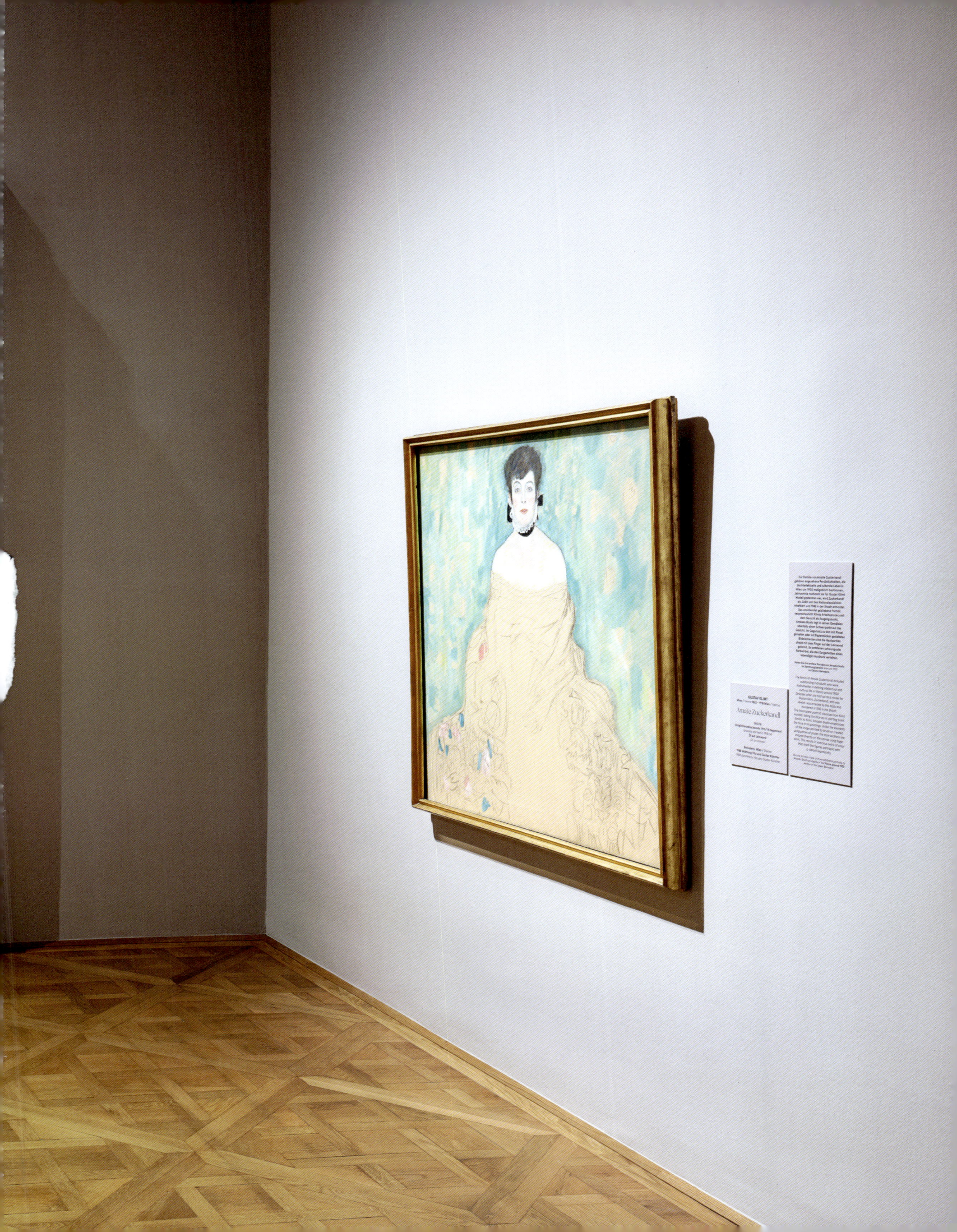

GUSTAV KLIMT
Wien / Vienna 1862 – 1918 Wien / Vienna
Amalie Zuckerkandl
1917/18
(möglicherweise bereits 1913/14 begonnen)
(possibly started in 1913–14)
Öl auf Leinwand
Oil on canvas
Belvedere, Wien / Vienna
1988 Widmung Vita und Gustav Künstler
1988 donated by Vita and Gustav Künstler
Zur Familie von Amalie Zuckerkandl gehören angesehene Persönlichkeiten, die das intellektuelle und kulturelle Leben in Wien um 1900 maßgeblich bestimmen. Jahrzehnte nachdem sie für Gustav Klimt Modell gestanden war, wird Zuckerkandl als Jüdin von den Nationalsozialisten inhaftiert und 1942 in der Shoah ermordet. Das unvollendet gebliebene Porträt veranschaulicht Klimts Arbeitsprozess mit dem Gesicht als Ausgangspunkt. Amoako Boafo legt in seinen Gemälden ebenfalls einen Schwerpunkt auf das Gesicht. Im Gegensatz zu den mit Pinsel gemalten oder mit Papierstücken gestalteten Bildelementen sind die Hautpartien direkt mit dem Finger auf der Leinwand geformt. So entstehen schwungvolle Farbwirbel, die den Dargestellten einen lebendigen Ausdruck verleihen.
Sehen Sie drei weitere Porträts von Amoako Boafo im Sammlungsbereich Wien um 1900 in Oberen Belvedere.
The family of Amalie Zuckerkandl included outstanding individuals who were instrumental in defining intellectual and cultural life in Vienna around 1900. Decades after she had sat as a model for Gustav Klimt, Zuckerkandl, who was Jewish, was arrested by the Nazis and murdered in 1942 in the Shoah. The incomplete portrait visualizes how Klimt worked, taking the face as his starting point. Similar to Klimt, Amoako Boafo emphasizes the face in his paintings. Unlike the elements of the image painted by brush or created using pieces of paper, the main sections are shaped directly on the canvas using finger work. This results in vivacious swirls of color that instil the figures portrayed with a vibrant expressivity.
Be sure to have a look at three additional portraits by Amoako Boafo on display in the Vienna around 1900 section of the upper Belvedere.

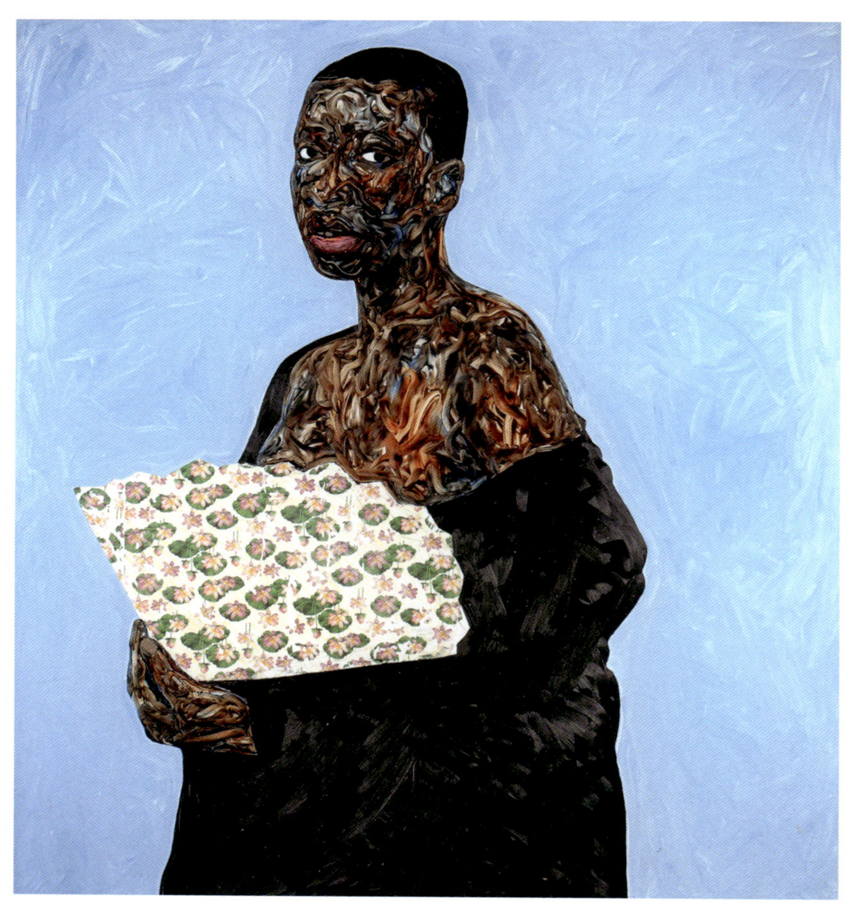

Belinda Ade Kazeem-Kamiński with a Purple Lily Fan
2019

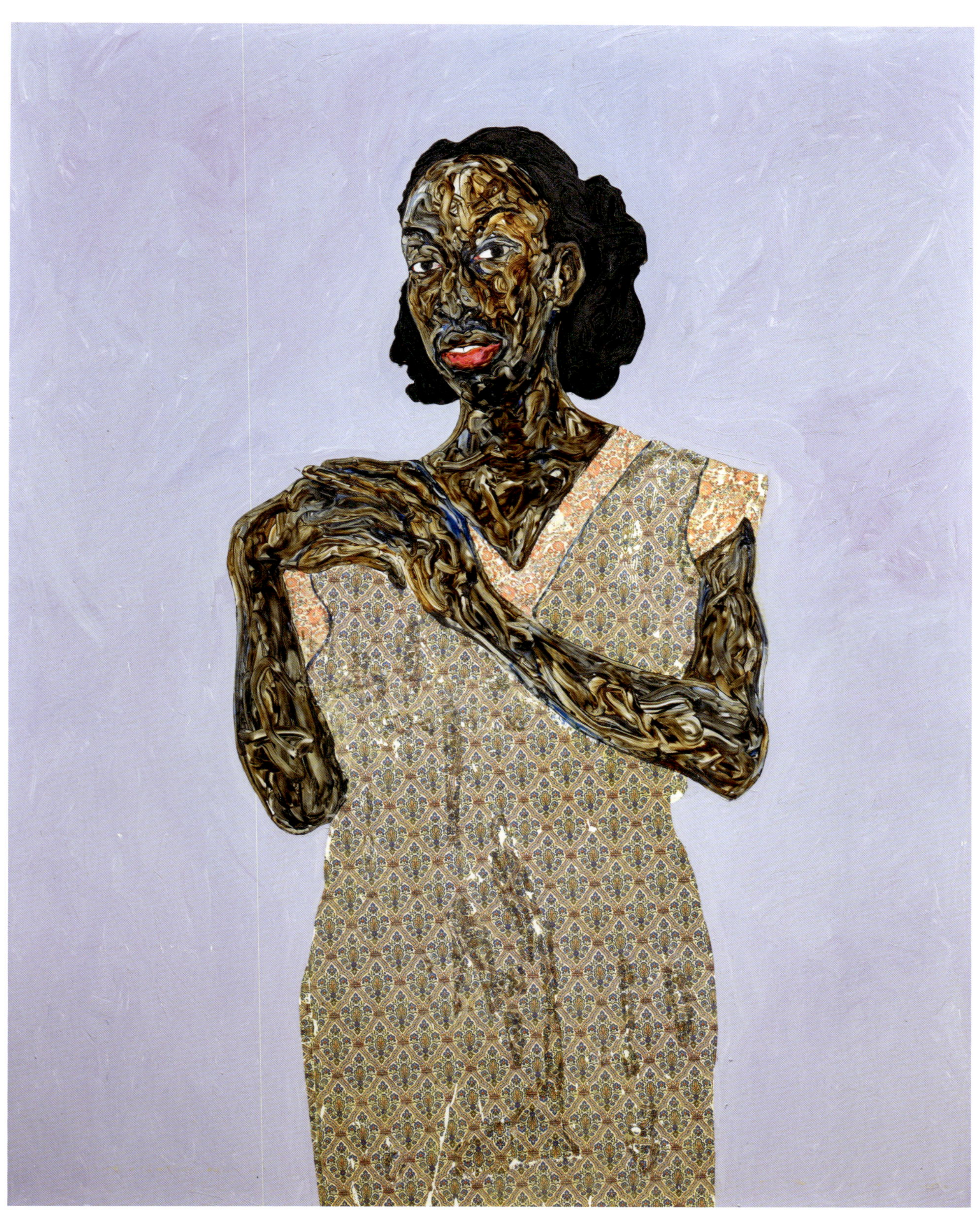

Abiona Esther Ojo
2019

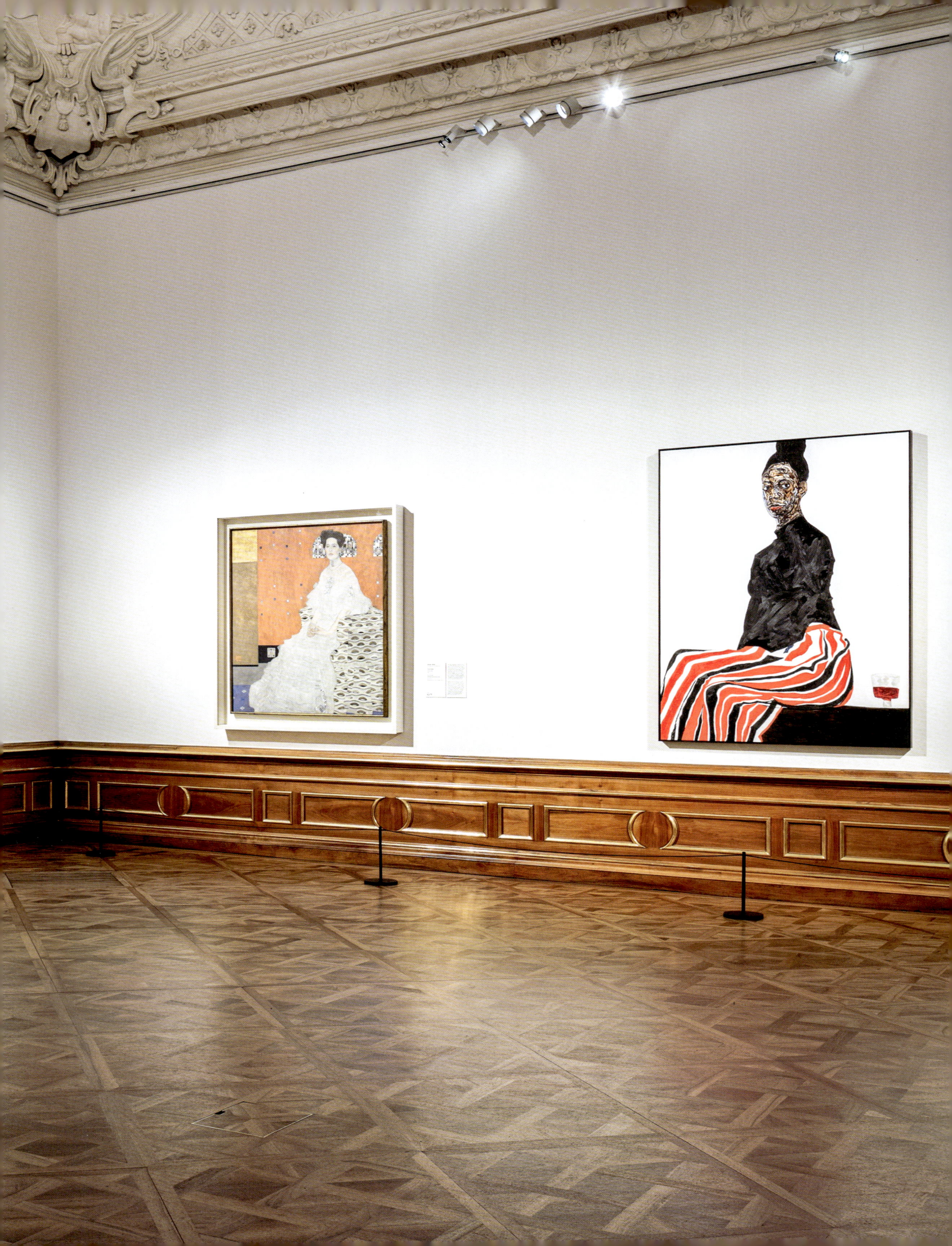

Amoako Boafo rose to international fame in 2019 with his portraits of friends and acquaintances from the Austrian Black community that borrow stylistically from Viennese Modernism. *Joy Adenike* shows feminist activist Joy Adenike Breiner, who champions the rights specifically of Black girls and women in Austria as part of the Schwarze Frauen Community organization and whom Boafo got to know during his time studying at the Academy of Fine Arts Vienna. Fashionably dressed and sitting upright, Breiner is presented as a three-quarter figure seated on a piece of black furniture, with a glass of red wine next to her. She looks straight out at the viewer in a leisurely fashion. Boafo has used his characteristic finger-painting technique to create her face. The texture of the skin clearly sets the almost sculptural figure off from the monochromatic white background created with broad brushstrokes, ensuring that Breiner becomes the central theme.

When staging and positioning his figures in the pictorial space, Boafo often takes his cue from Gustav Klimt, the founder of Viennese Modernism. This is poignantly visualized in the Upper Belvedere with the juxtaposition of the portraits of *Joy Adenike* and *Fritza Riedler* (1906). Unlike Klimt's images, which depict women from upper-class Viennese society often in an idealized setting, the portraits Boafo paints of his contemporaries from the Austrian Black community attest to a self-determined image of Black identity and what it means to be a woman. Breiner is represented as a self-confident woman who resolutely lives in her body and seizes the space surrounding her.

Boafo paints people he knows personally and whose contribution to the Black diaspora he wishes to emphasize in his oeuvre. With the portrait of the Vienna activist, he indirectly references a key extension of feminist theory, Black feminism, which, as a political and social movement and unlike other feminist currents, highlights the specific forms of discrimination against and repression of Black girls and women. VS

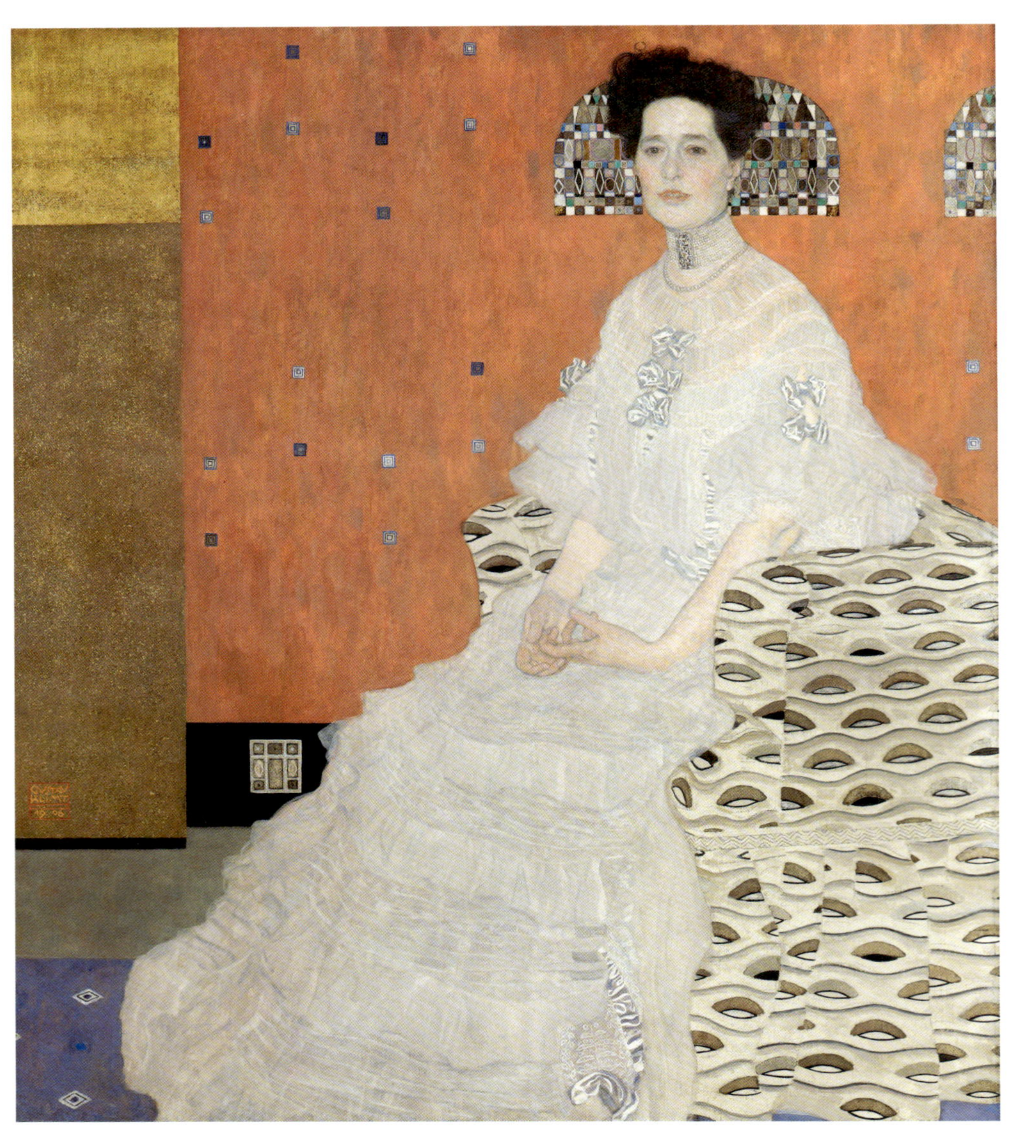

Gustav Klimt

Fritza Riedler
1906

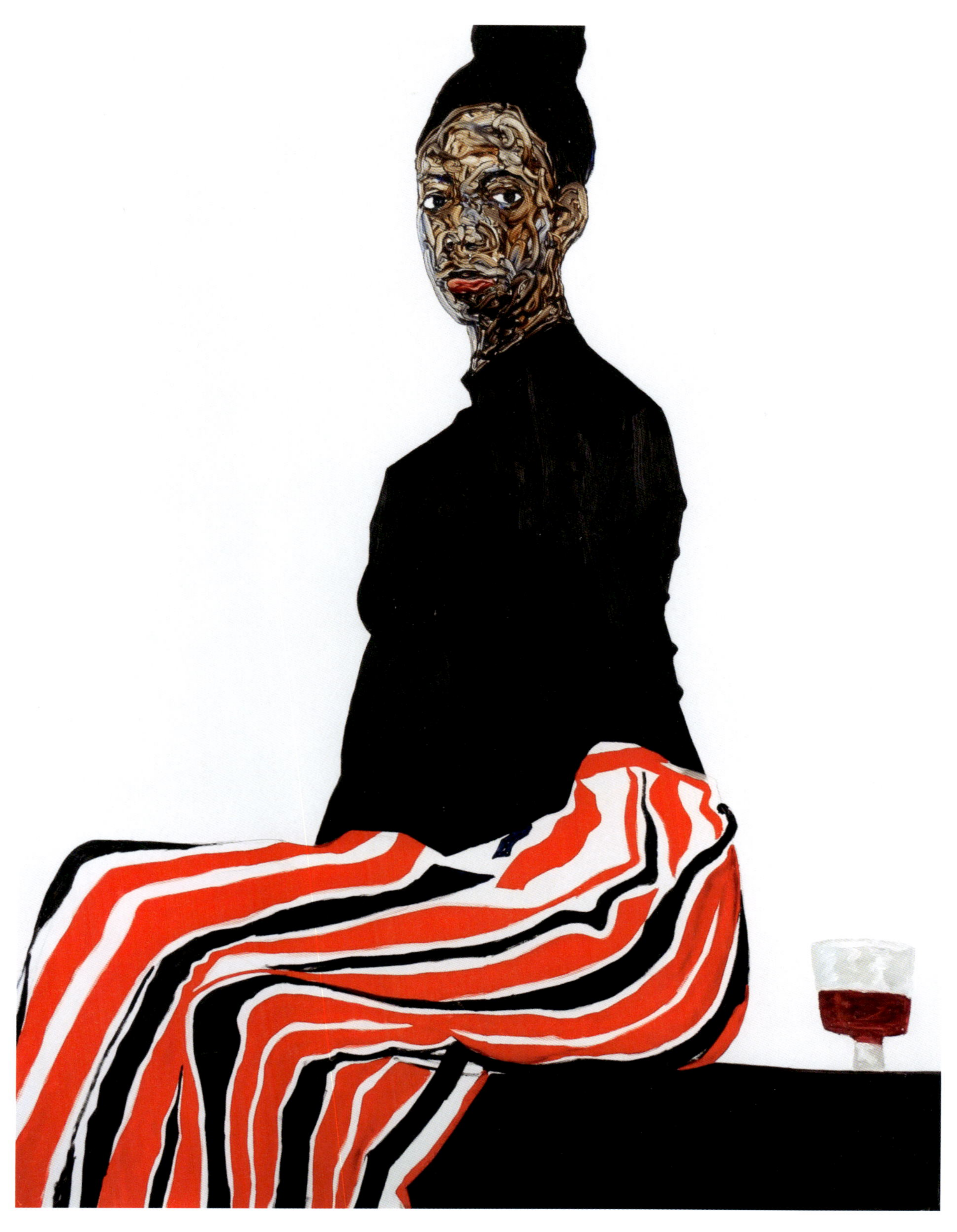

Joy Adenike
2019

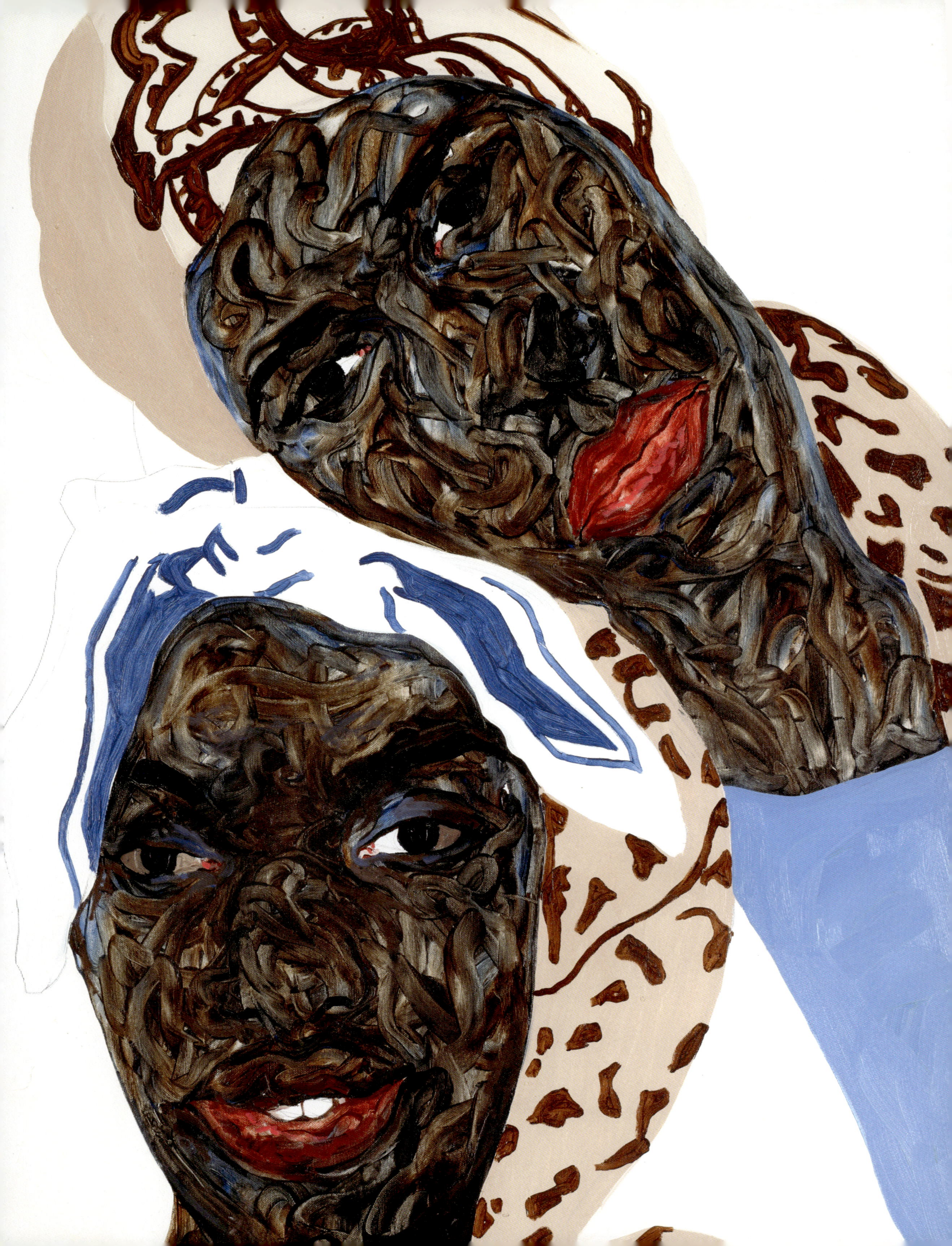

Proper Love

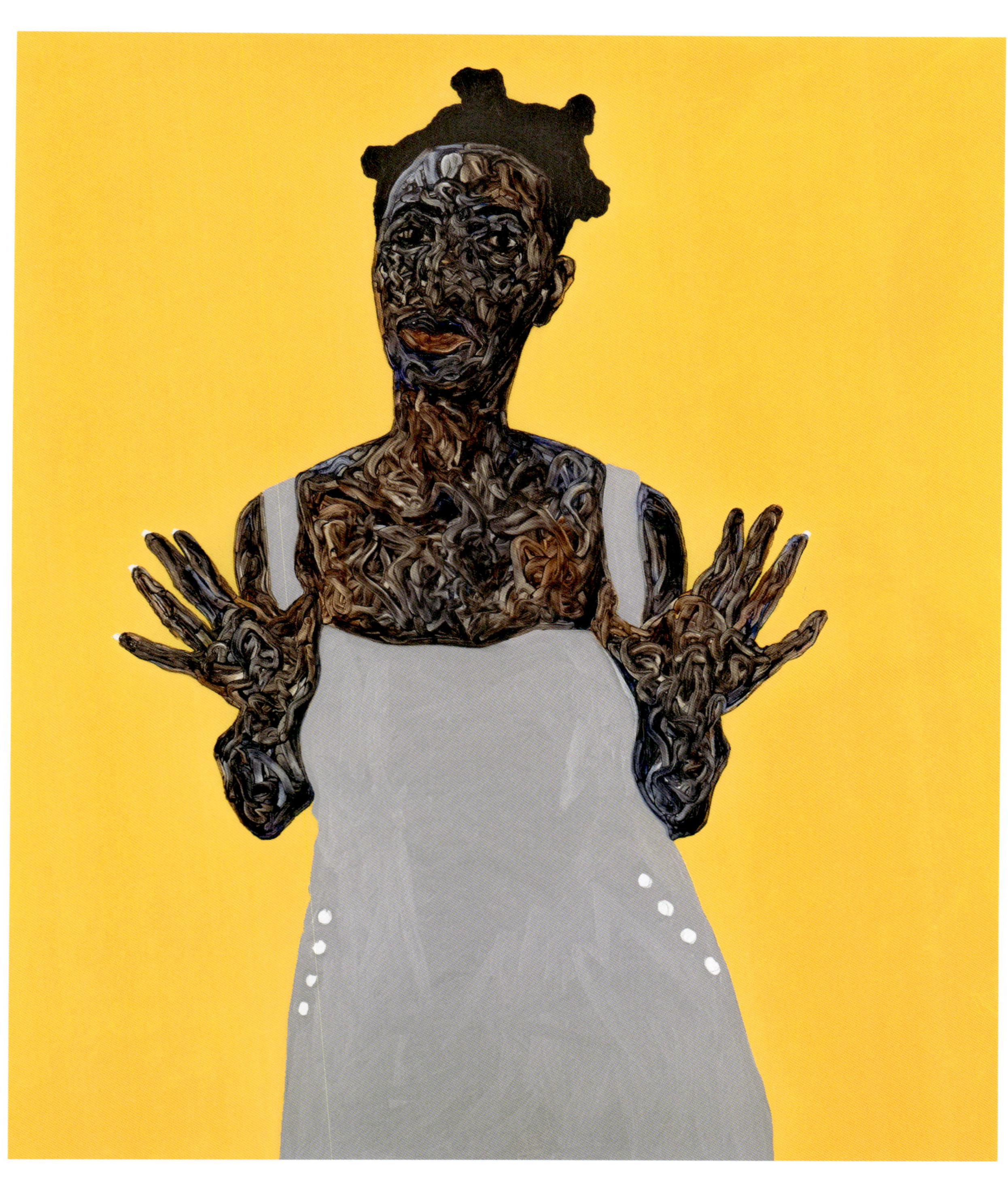

Silver Dungaree
2021

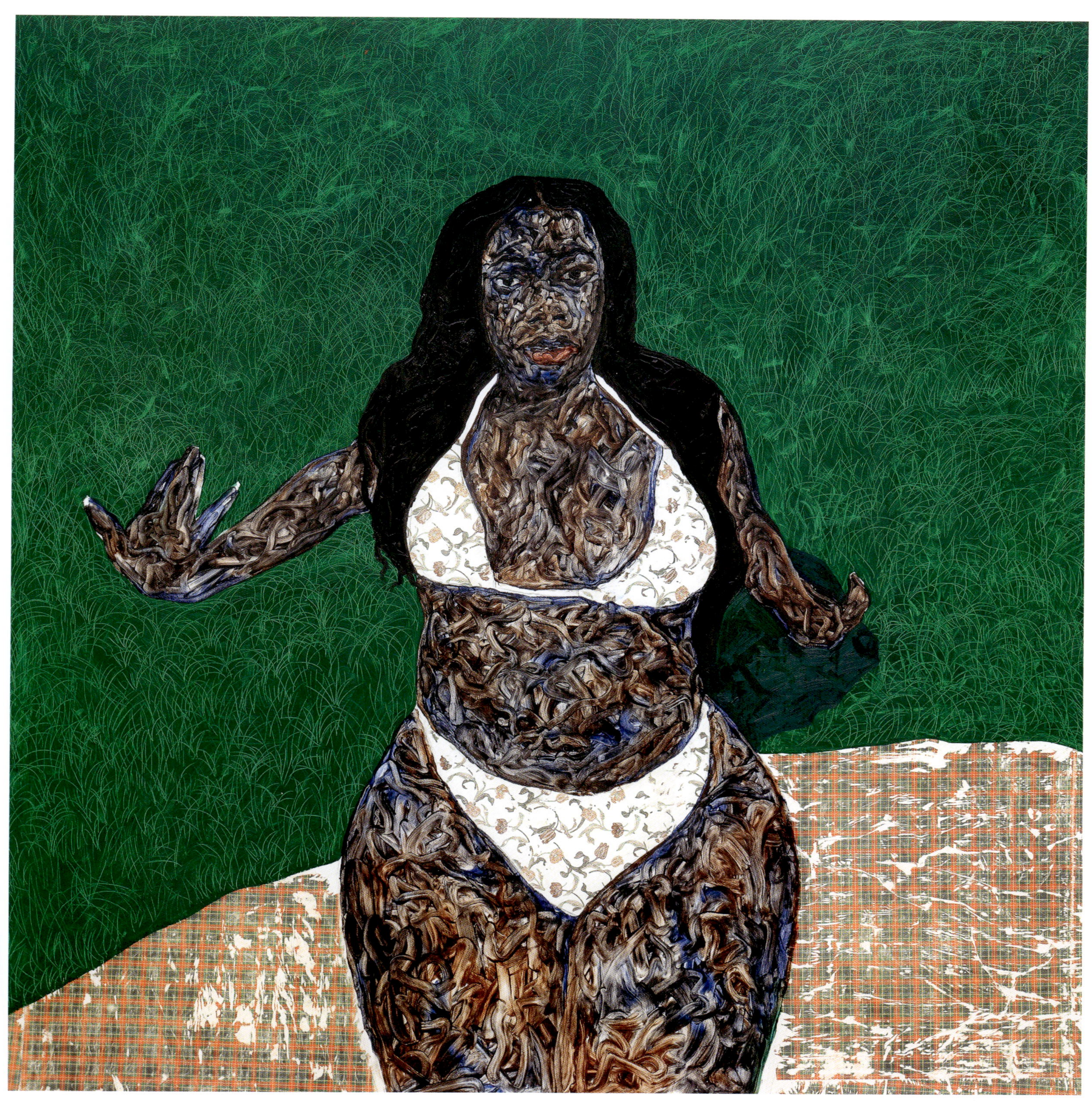

Rose Bikini

2022

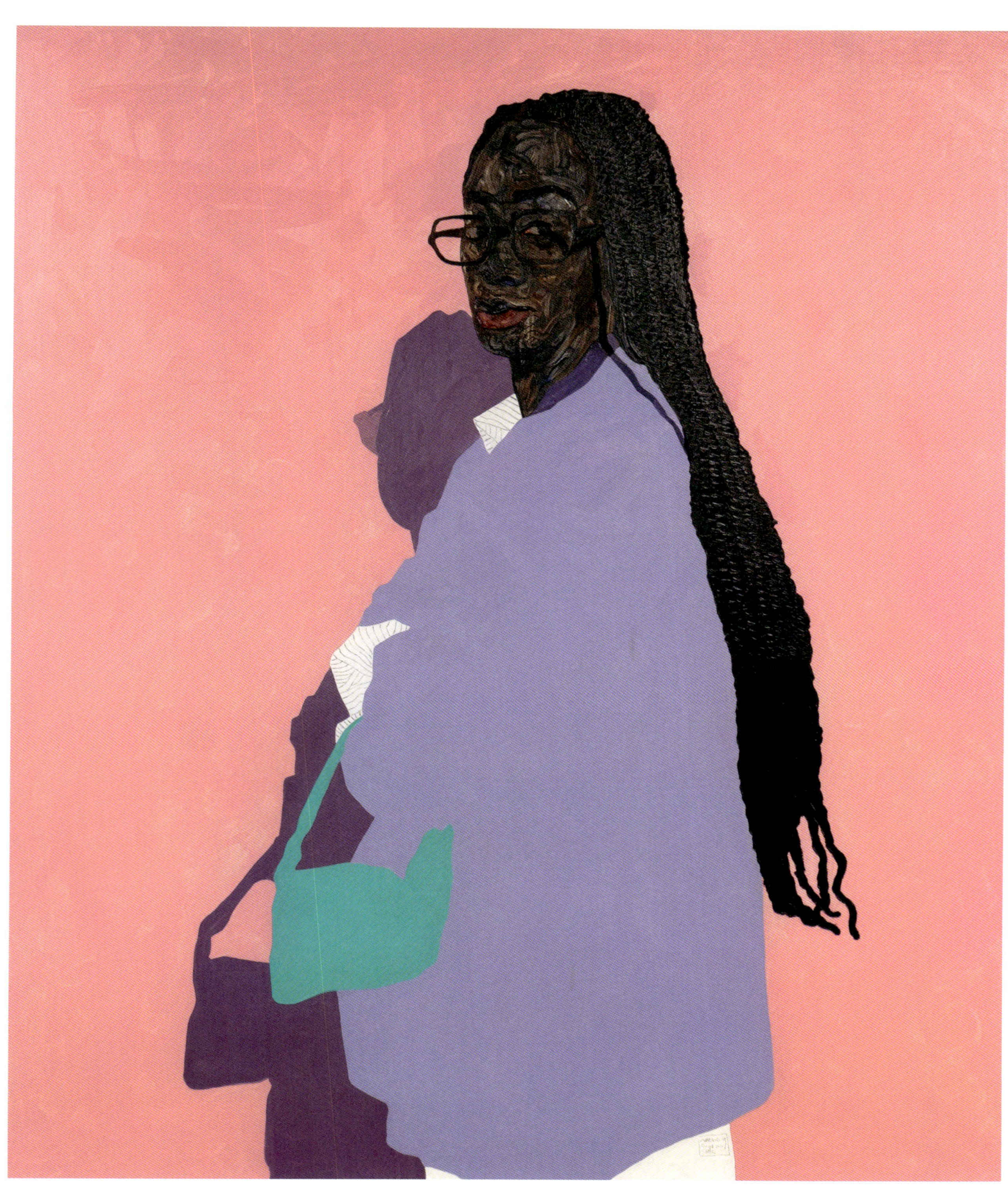

Green Handbag
2021

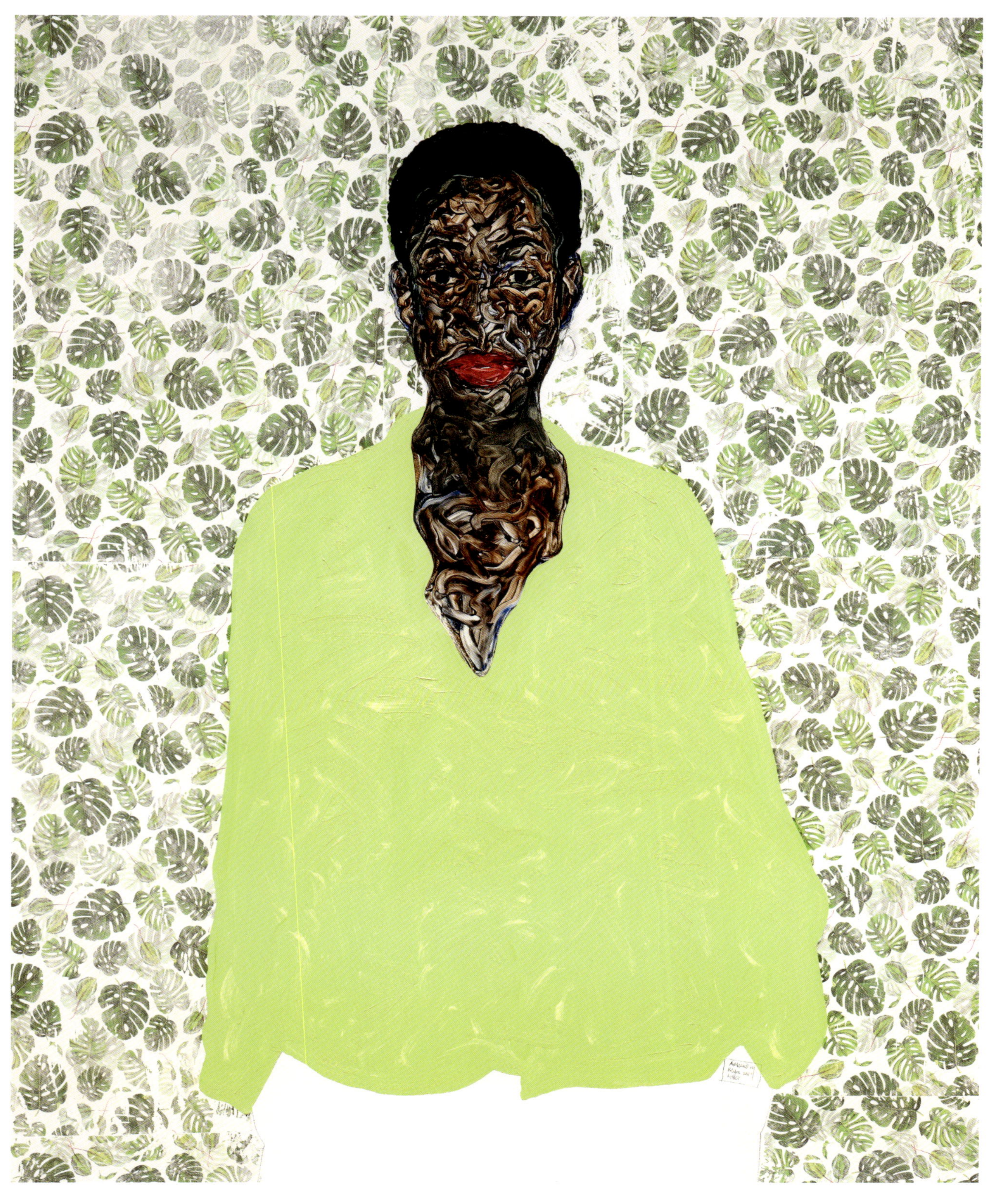

Monstera Leaf Background

2020

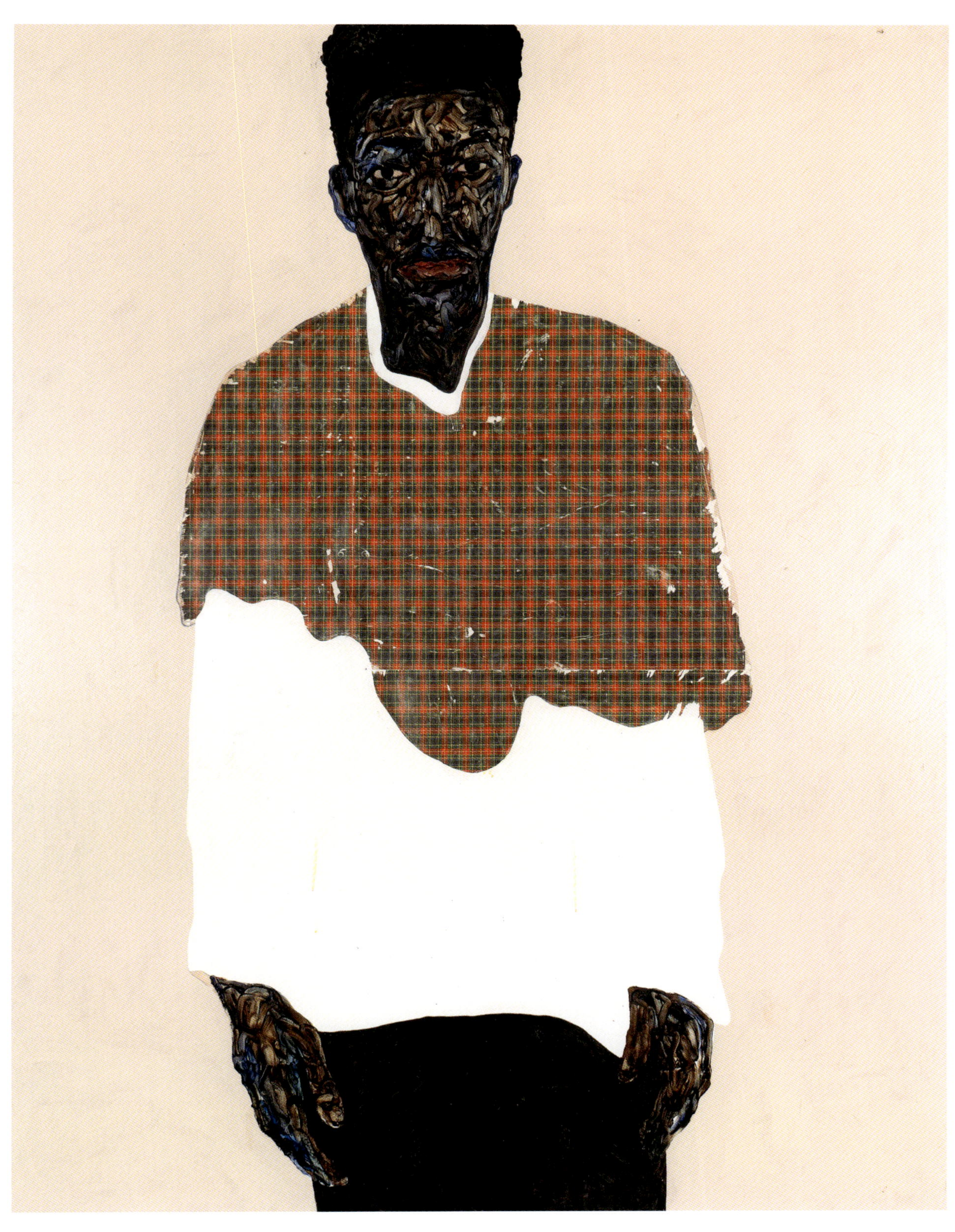

Checkered Mofler

2020

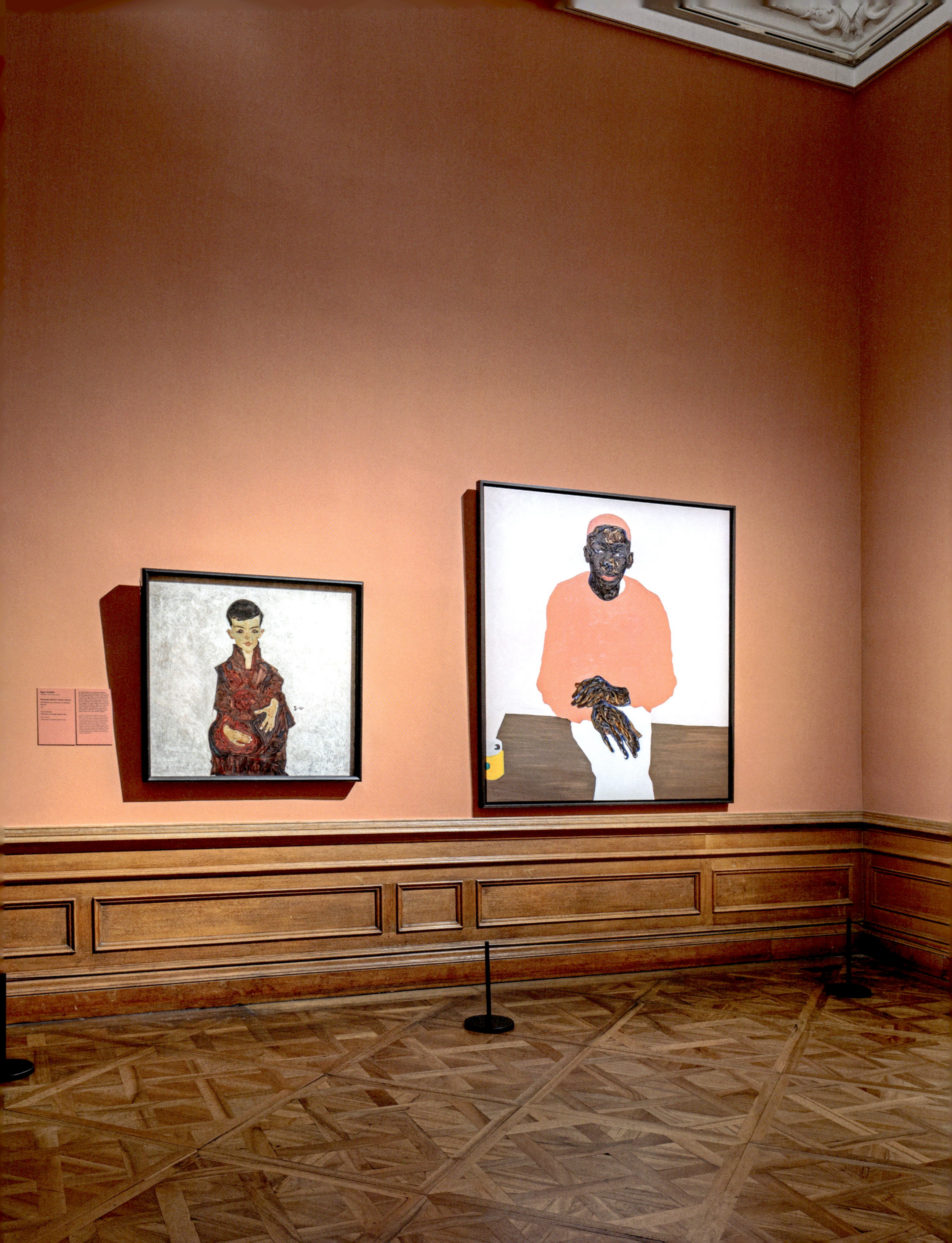

The full-figure portrait of French model, dancer, and fashion influencer Gregory Robert that Amoako Boafo painted in 2019 shows a young man sitting casually in an abstract interior and—as if staged for a fashion magazine—confidently looking at the viewer. An eye-catching element is his short hair, dyed pink to fashionably match the pink tone of his pullover. The technique with which Boafo molds the skin of his figures on the canvas reveals a sensually expressive aesthetic and an unmistakable formal language that he developed while studying in Vienna. Precisely this expressivity and the staging of the figures attests to the close links to role models from the days of Viennese Modernism such as Egon Schiele, as can be seen from the juxtaposition of *Gregory Robert* with Schiele's *Reiner Boy* (1910) in the Upper Belvedere. In both works, the dynamism stems primarily from the expressive hands of those portrayed. While the hands of five-year-old Herbert Reiner, the scion of an upper-class Viennese family, are unnaturally boney, Gregory Robert's seem veritably tender, underscoring his leisurely, elegant posture. In contrast to Schiele, Boafo relies on a colorful Pop palette in his oeuvre to lend expression to the emotional depth and personal identity of the figures. The carefully selected fashionable accessories and the individual appearance of the sitter are decisive narrative elements. In this portrait of the pink-clad fashion influencer, Boafo questions customary social stereotypes and instead paints a complex image of Black masculinity that incorporates vulnerability and sensitivity. VS

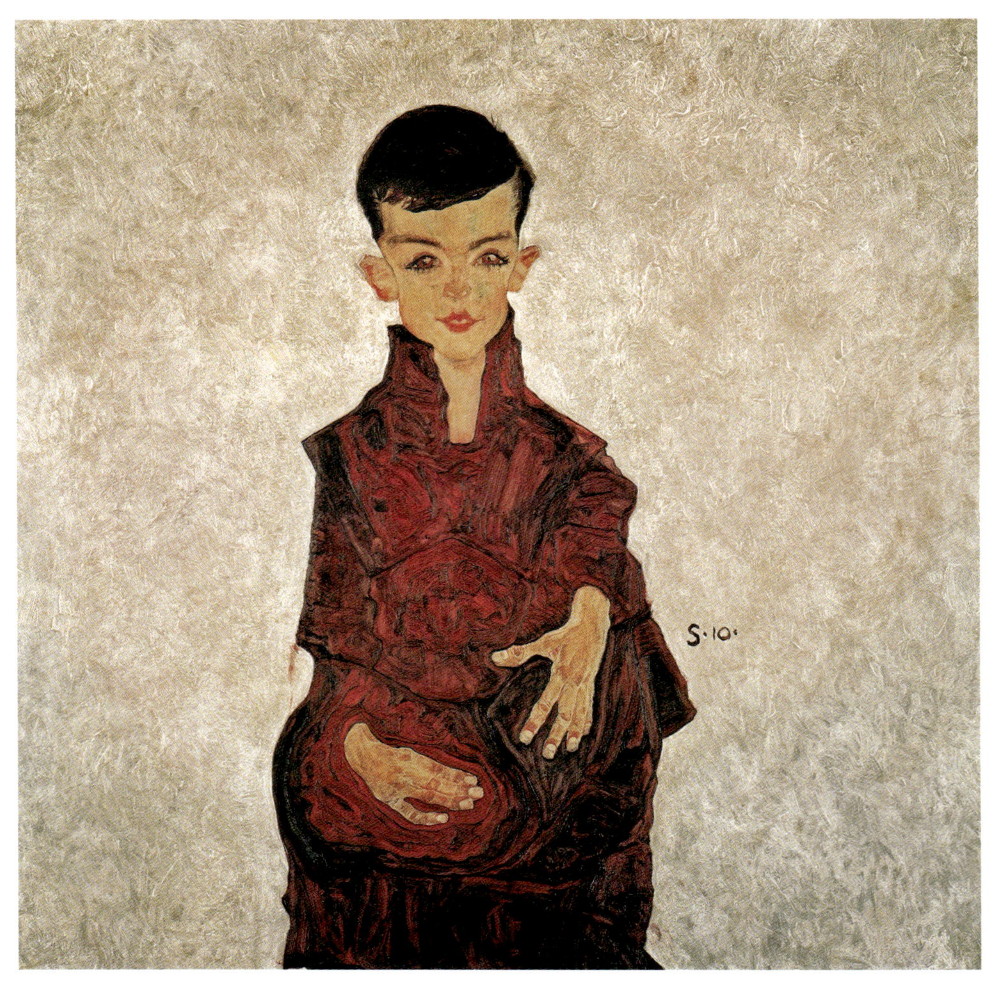

Egon Schiele

The Reiner Boy (Portrait of Herbert Reiner)
1910

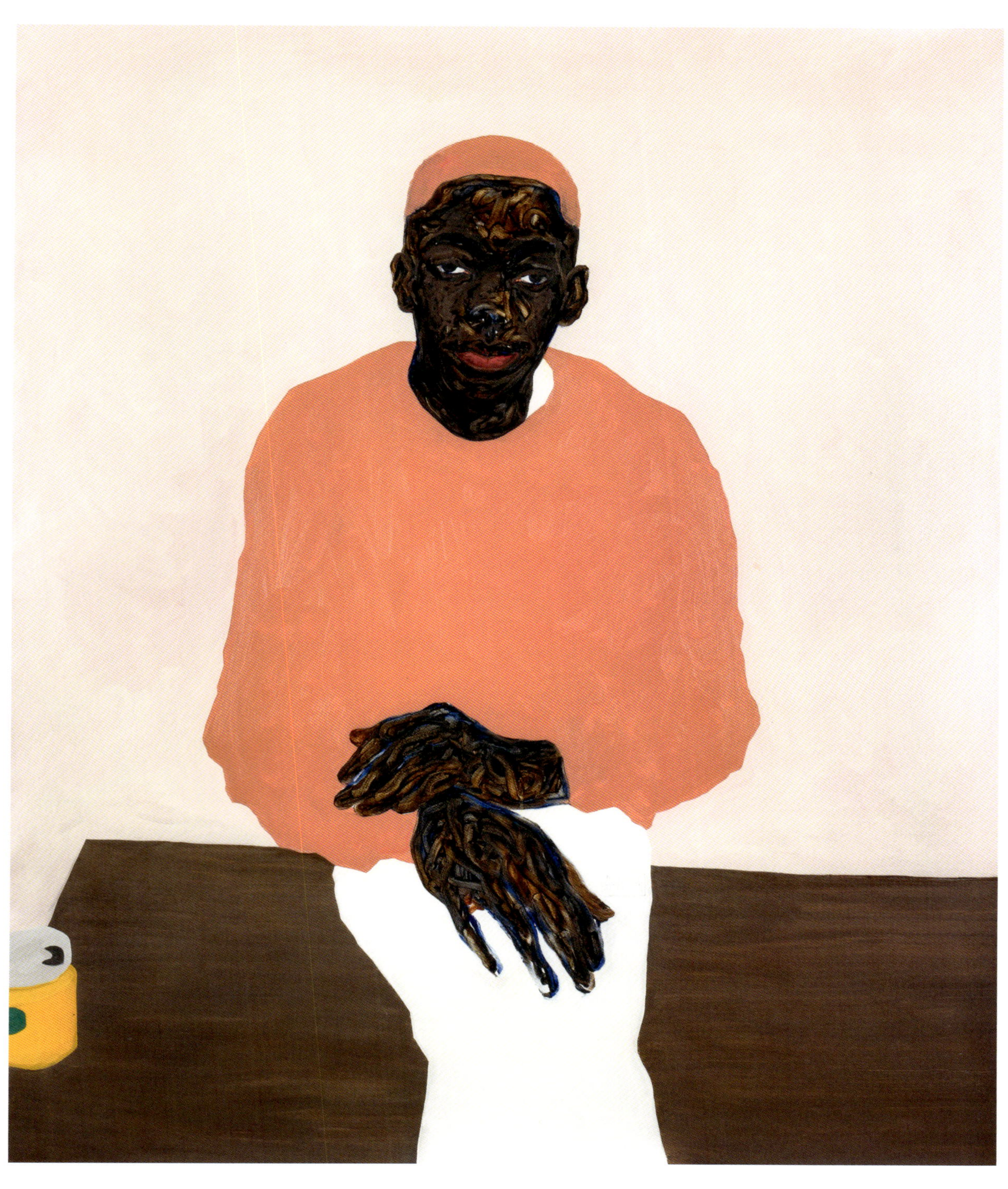

Gregory Robert
2019

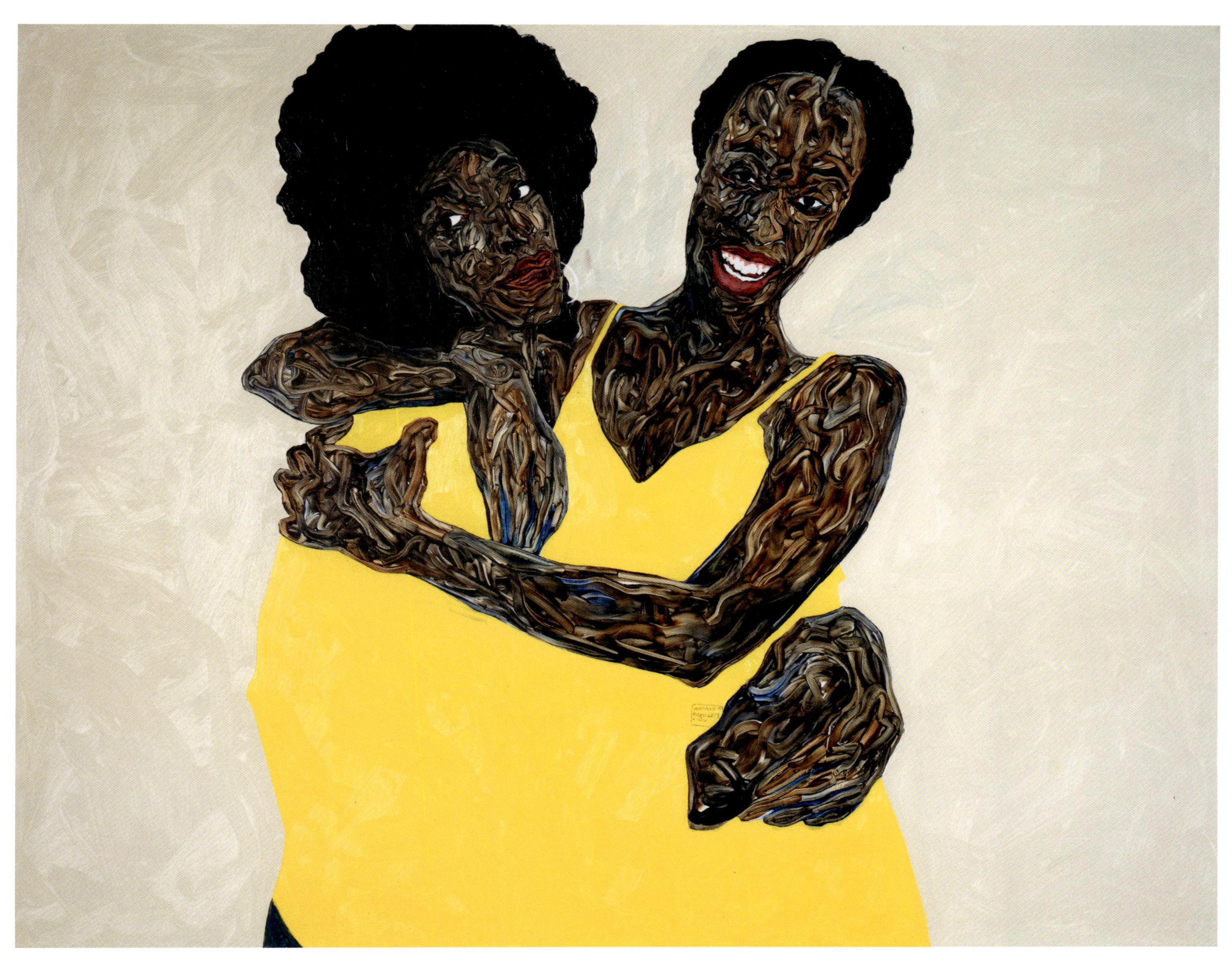

Huggers in Yellow
2019

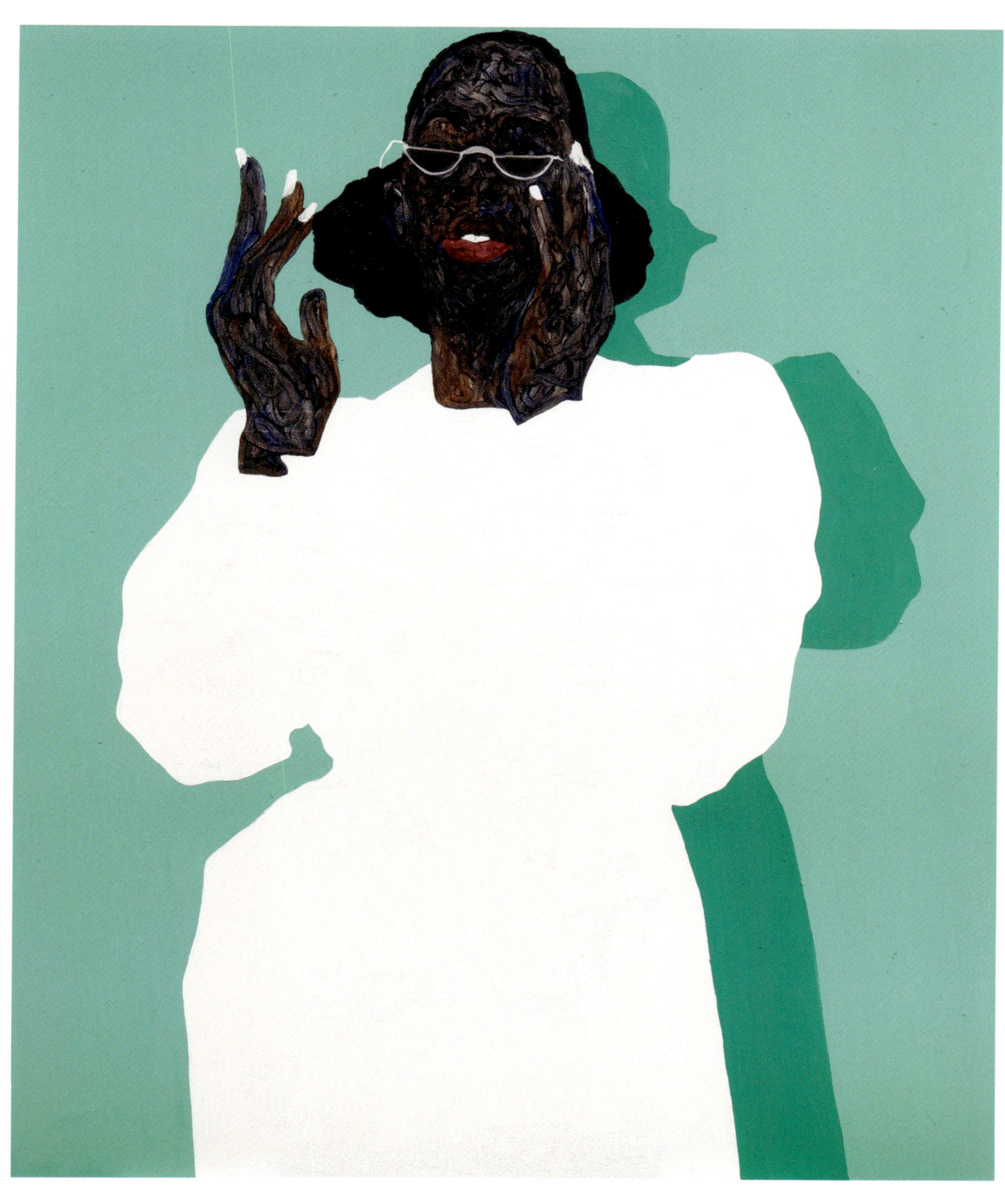

White Nail Polish
2021

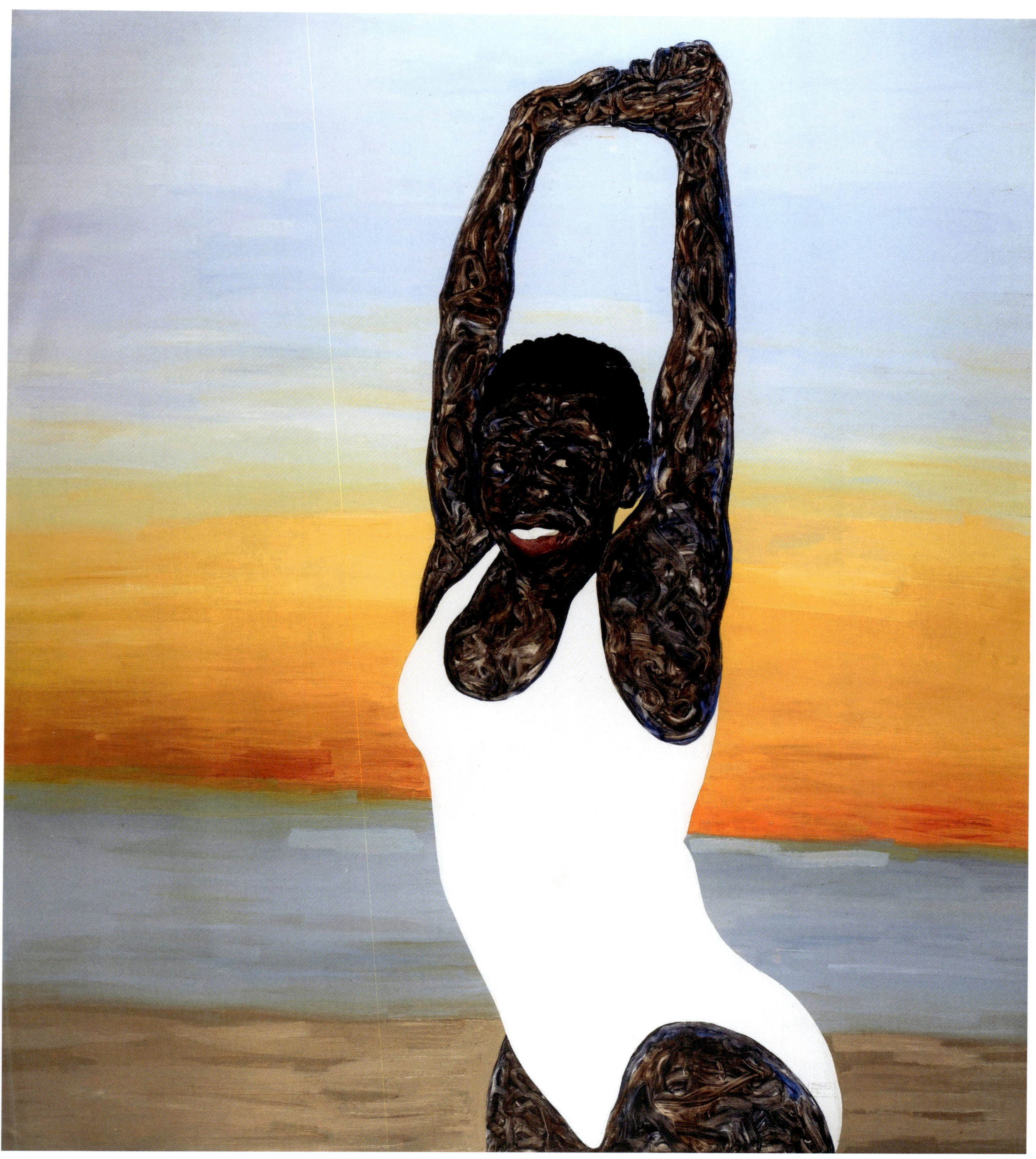

Sunset I
2021

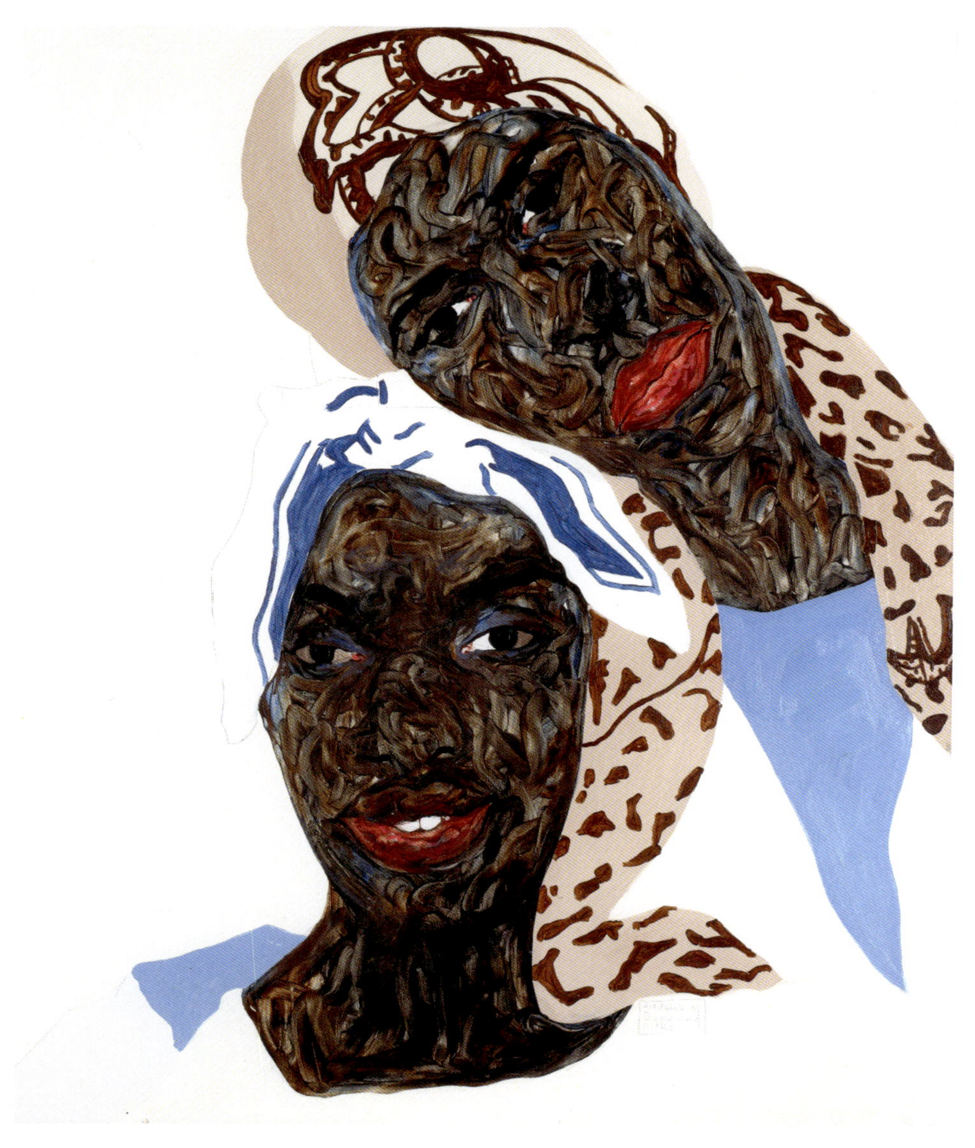

Touching Heads
2020

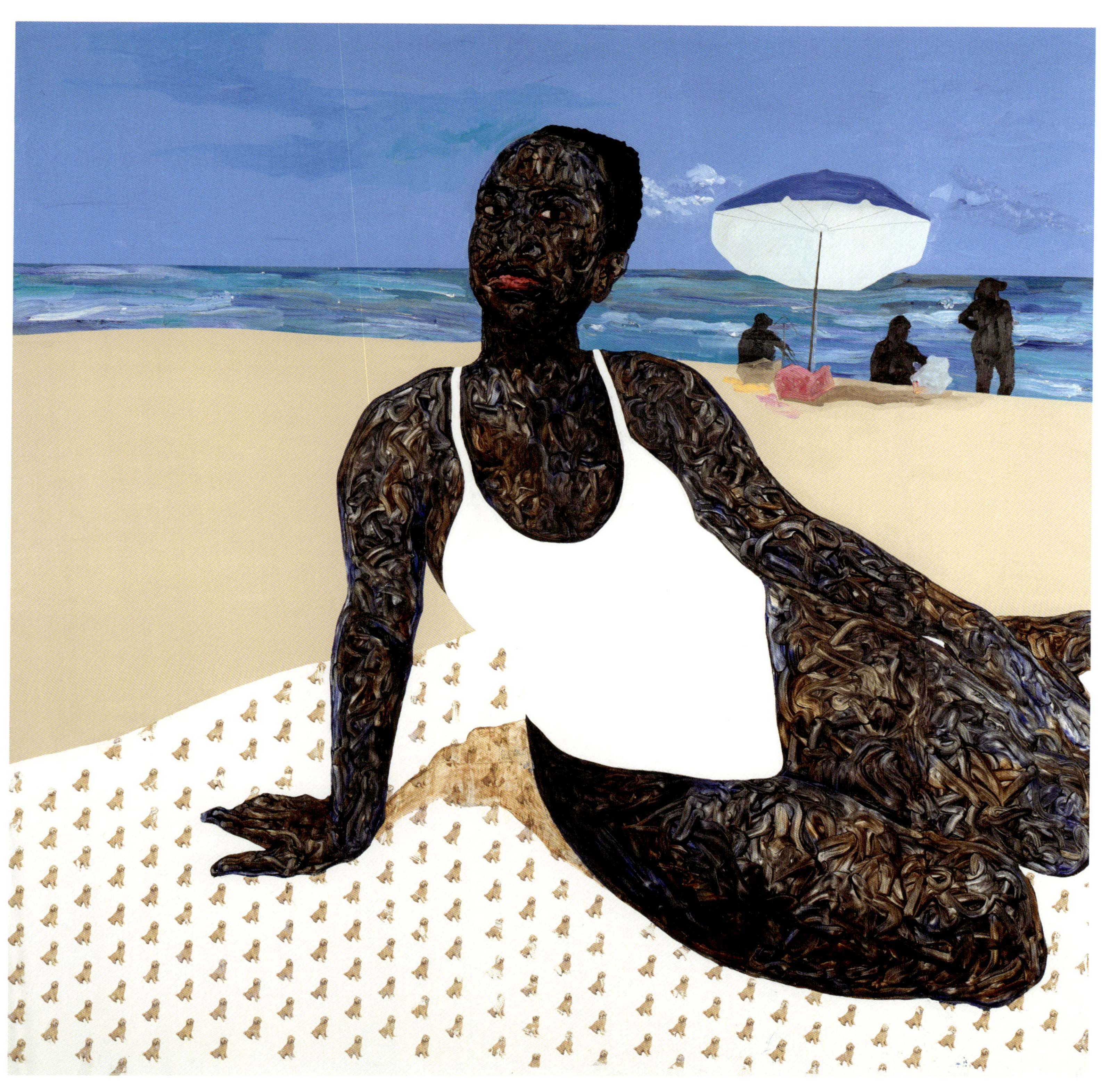

Puppy Blankie
2022

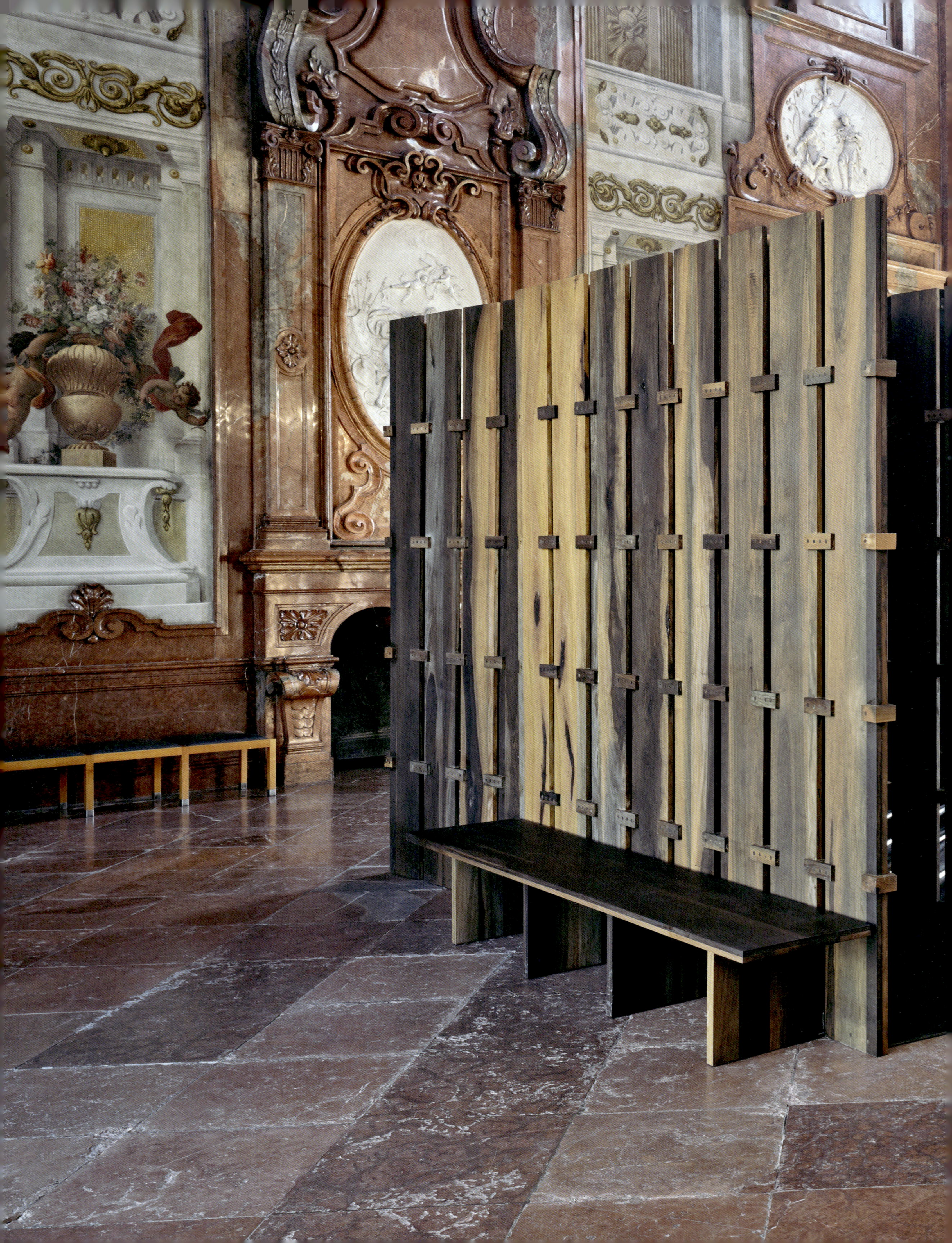

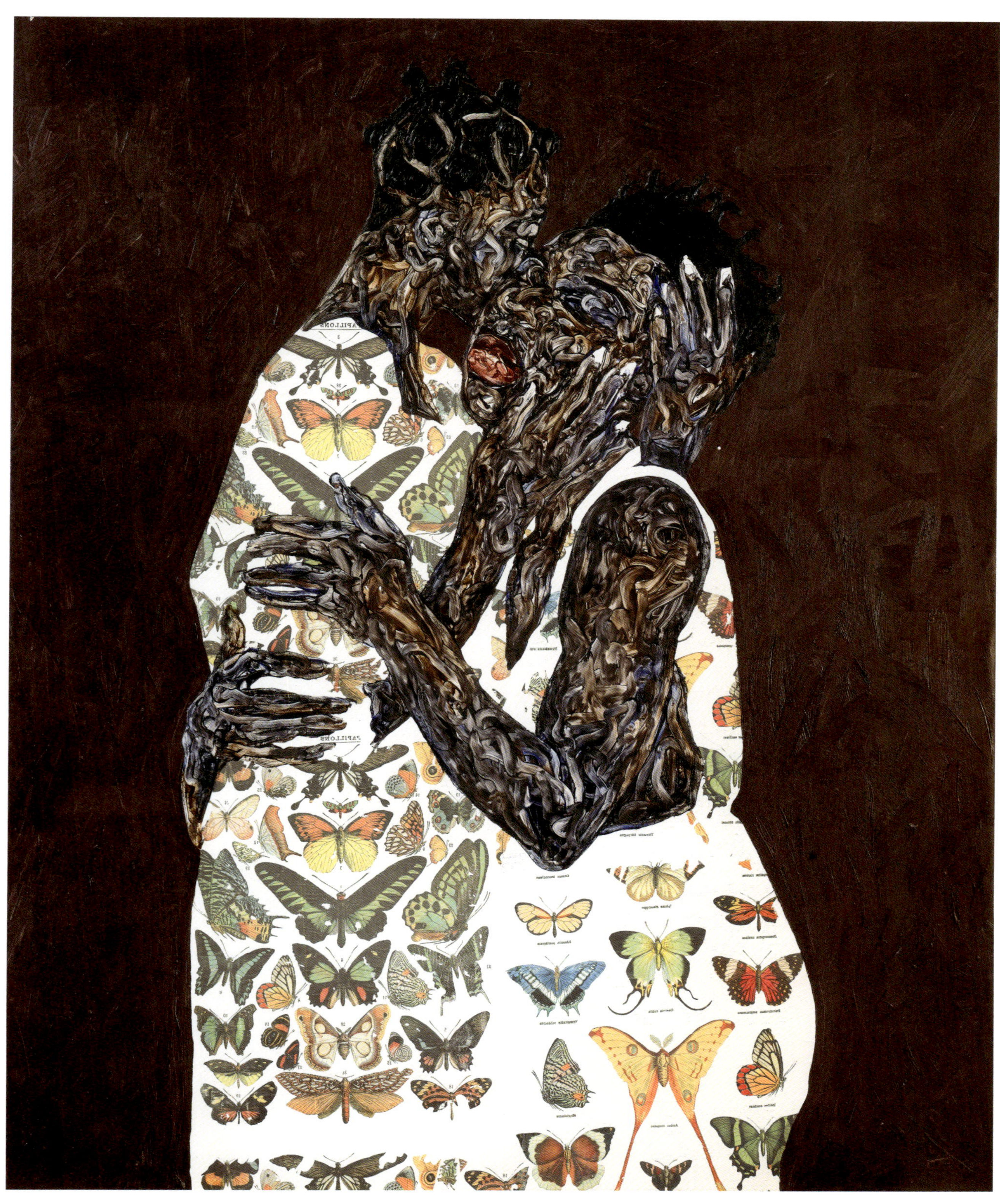

Papillon Hug
2023

Volta Pavillon
2024

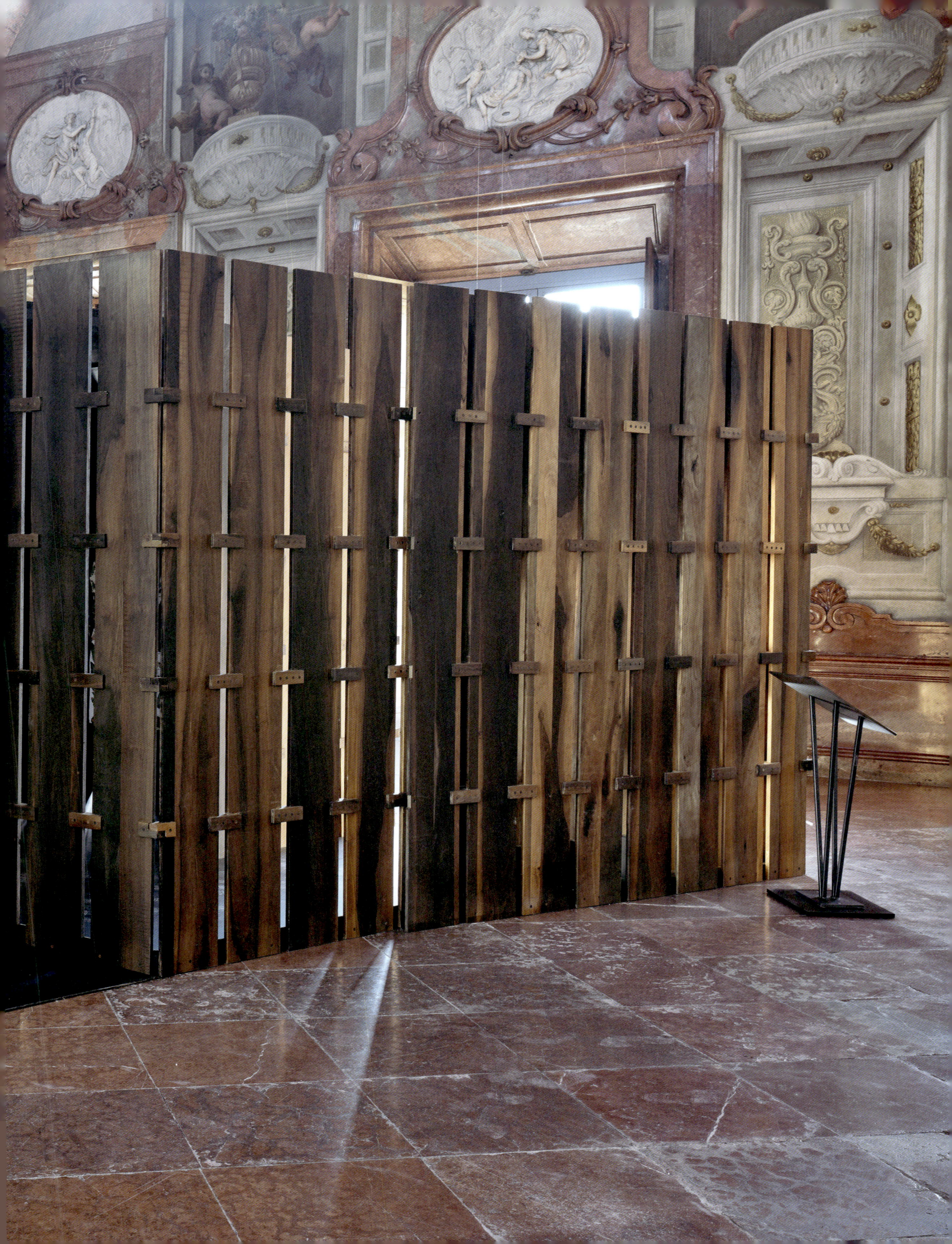

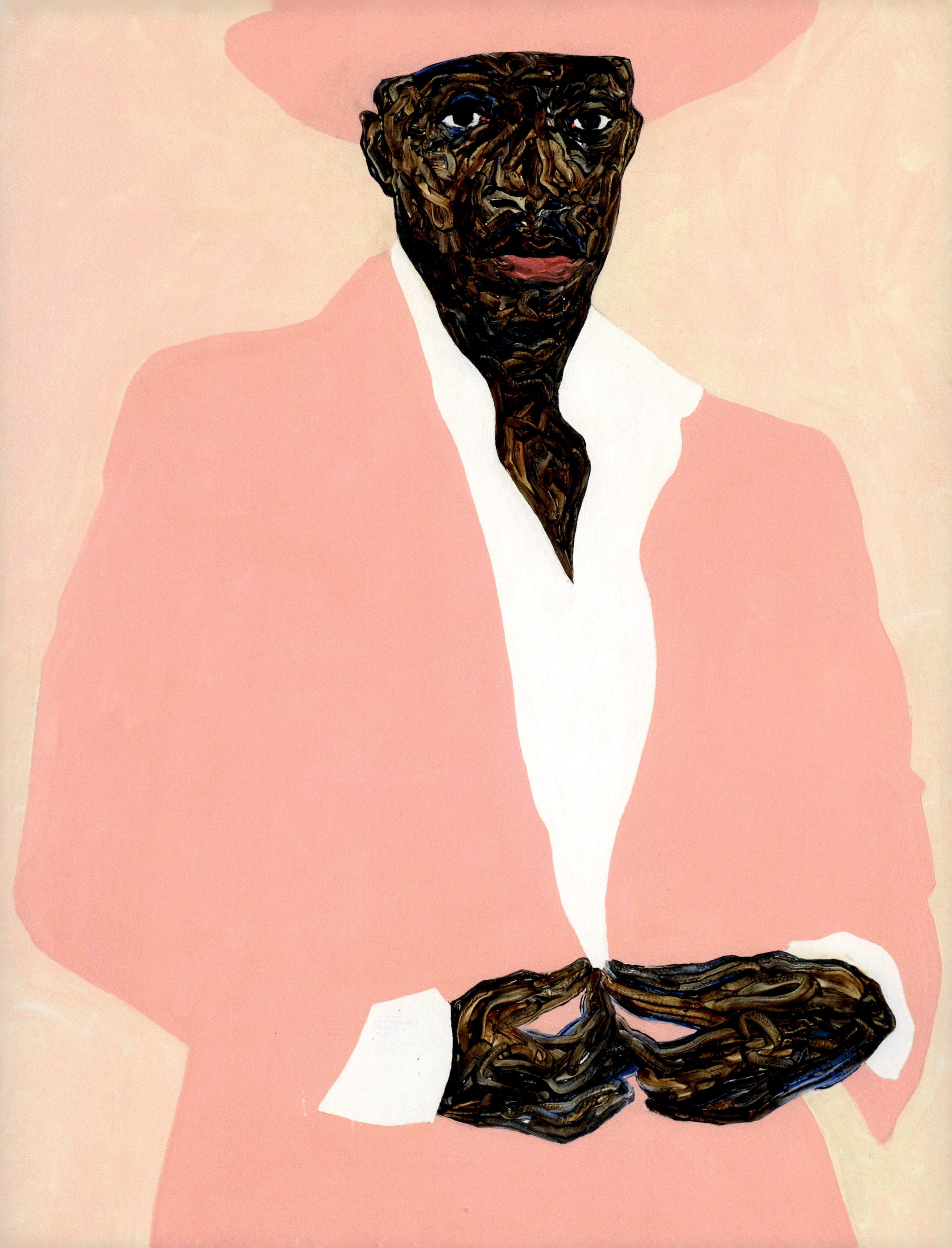

Masculinities

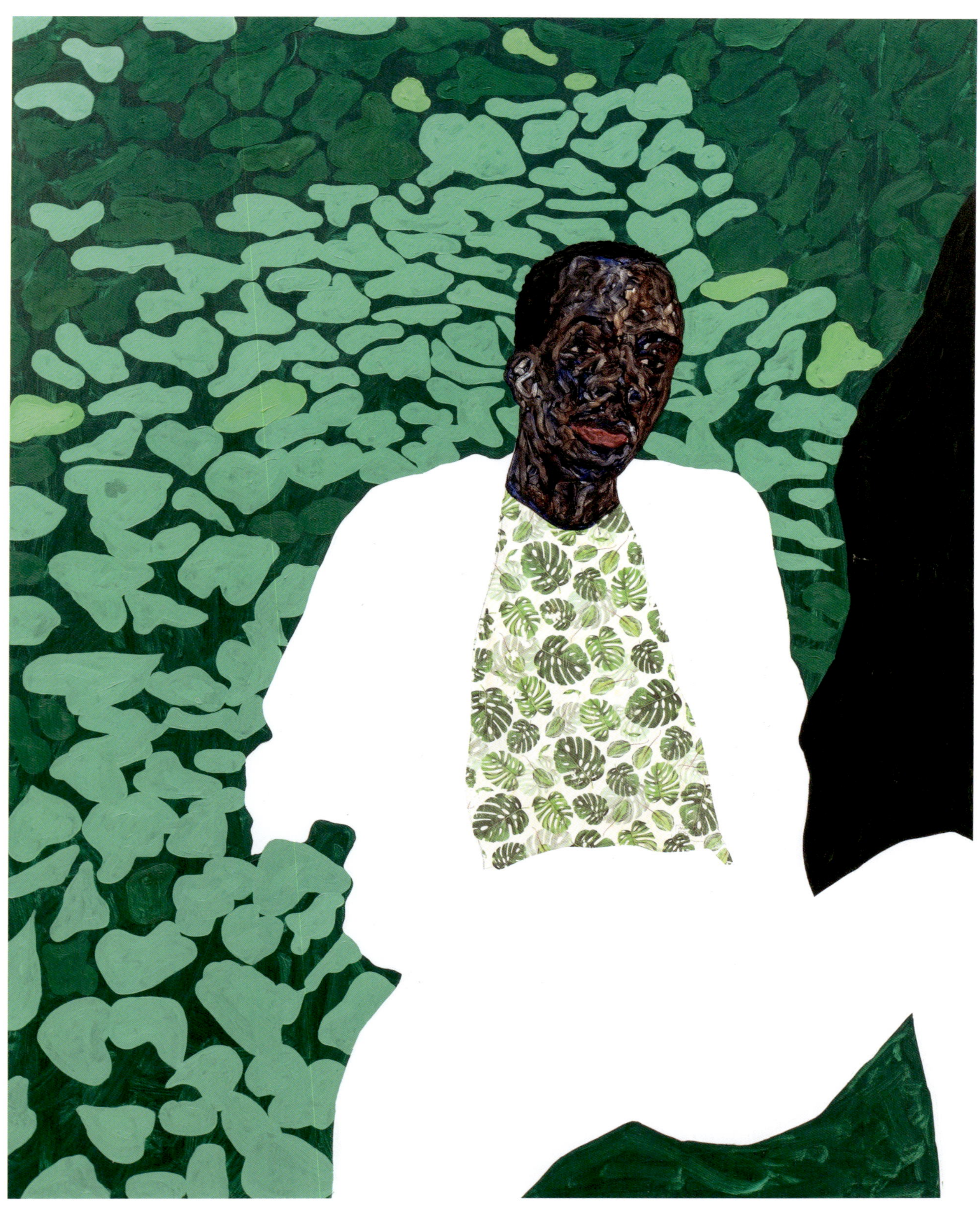

Green Petals

2022

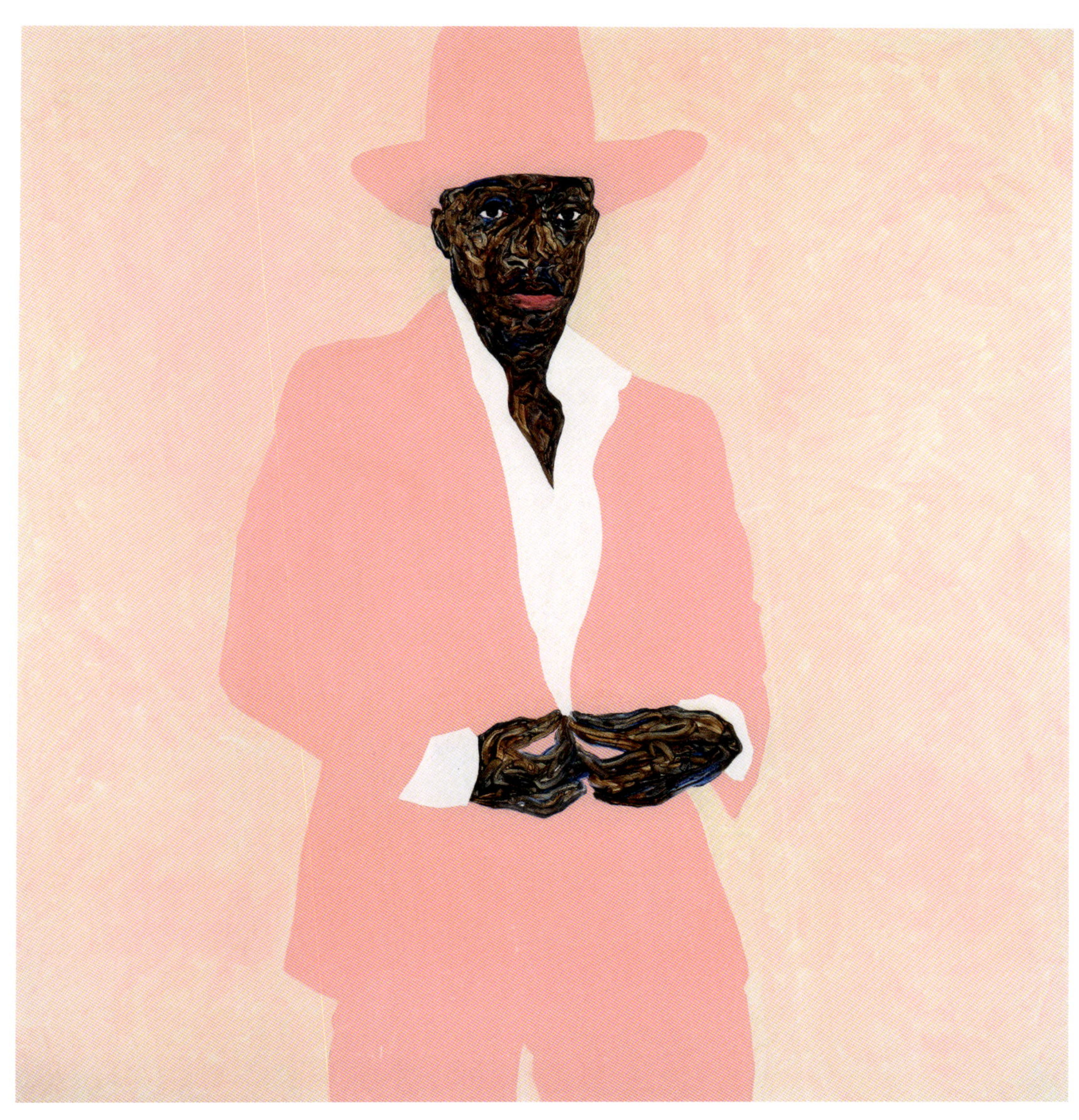

Pink Hat
2019

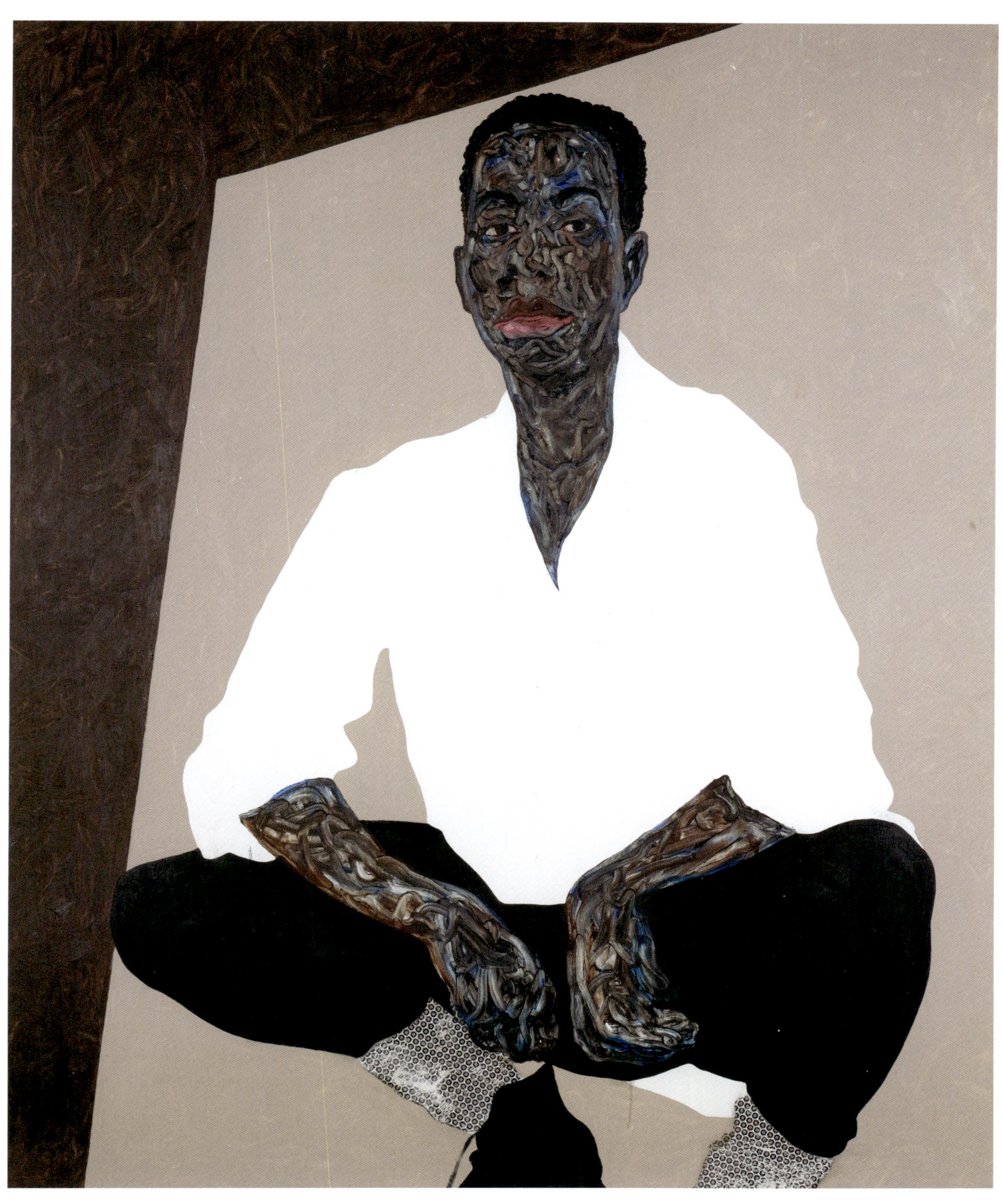

Black Pants

2020

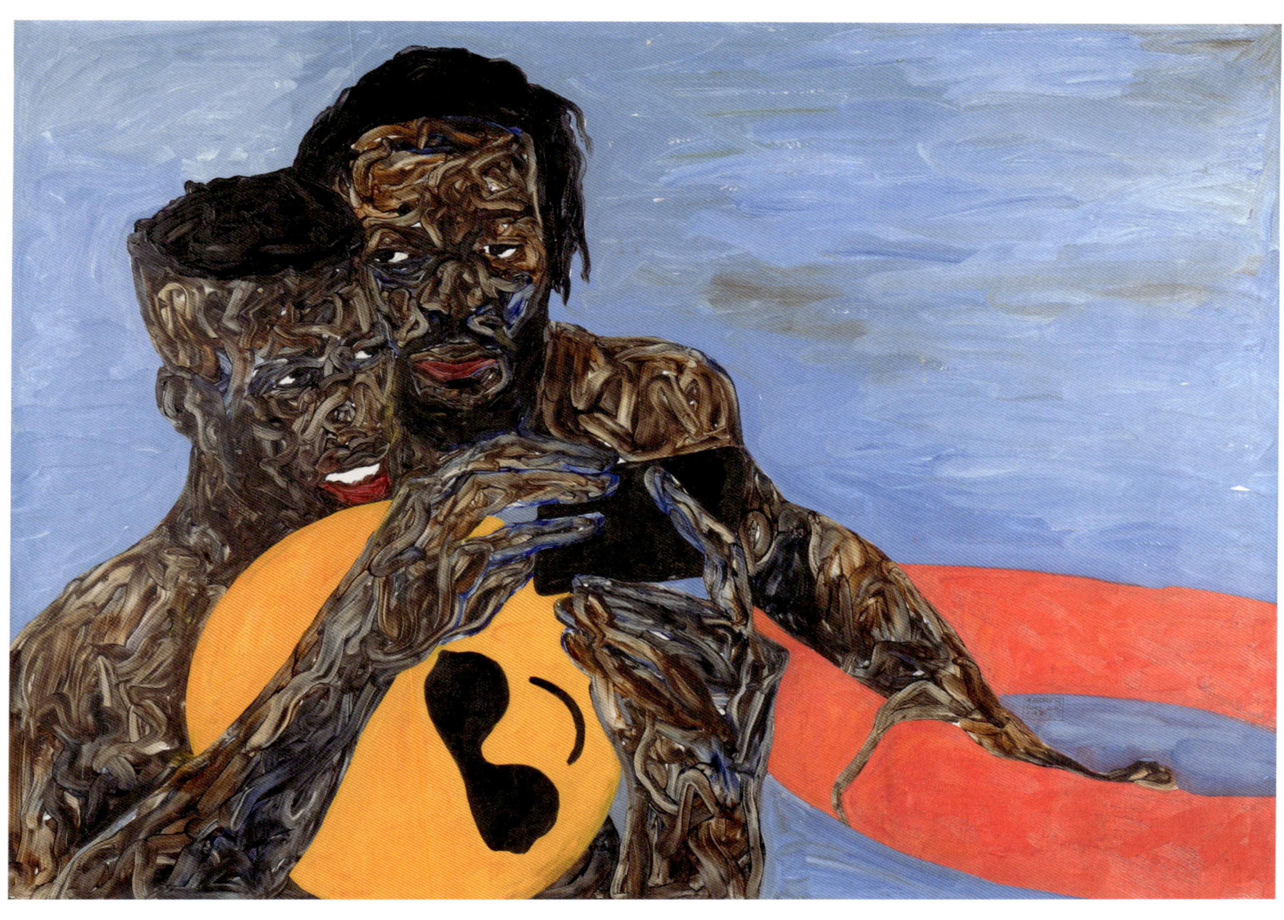

Mr. Palm with the Yellow Ball
2019

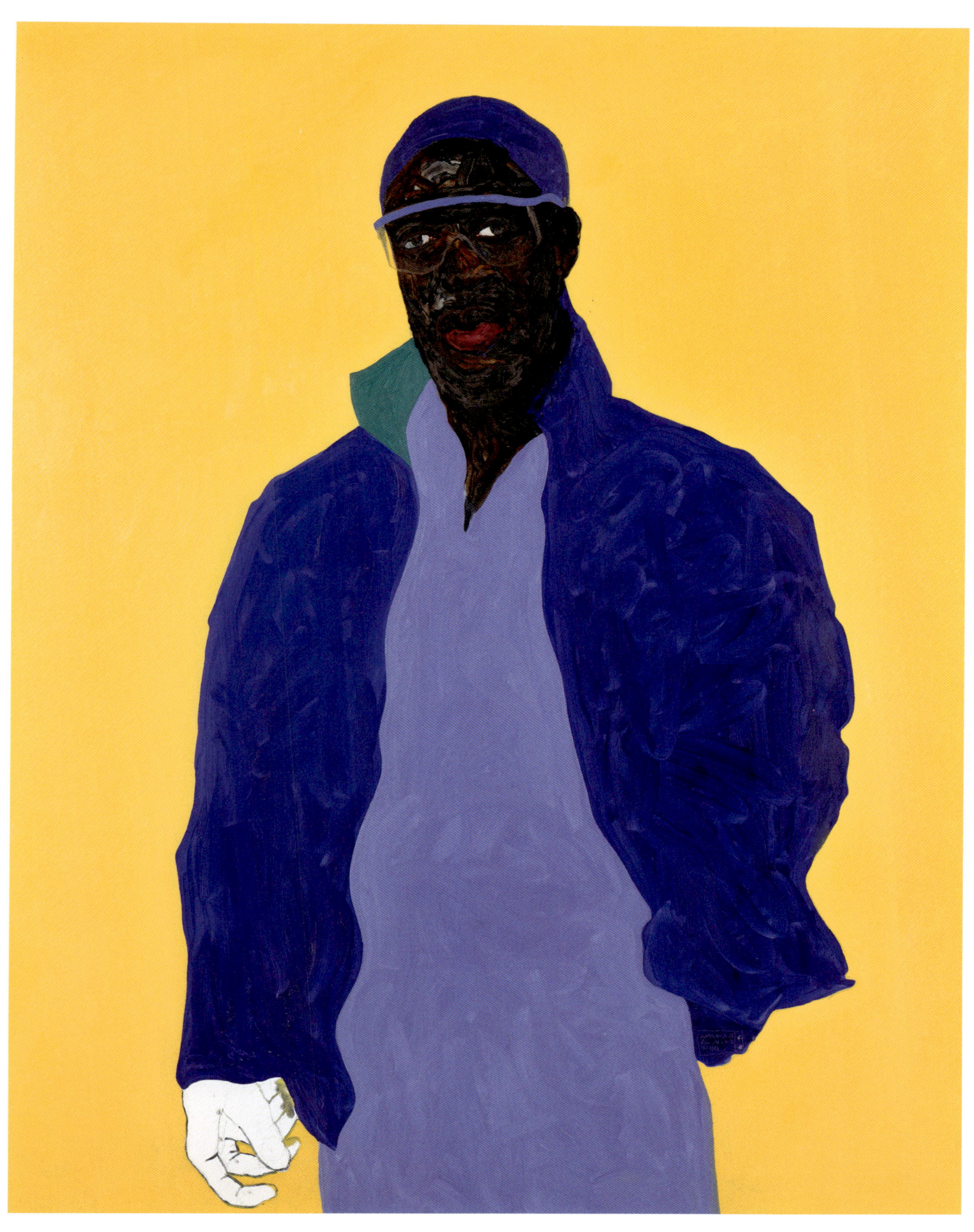

Steve Mekoudja
2019

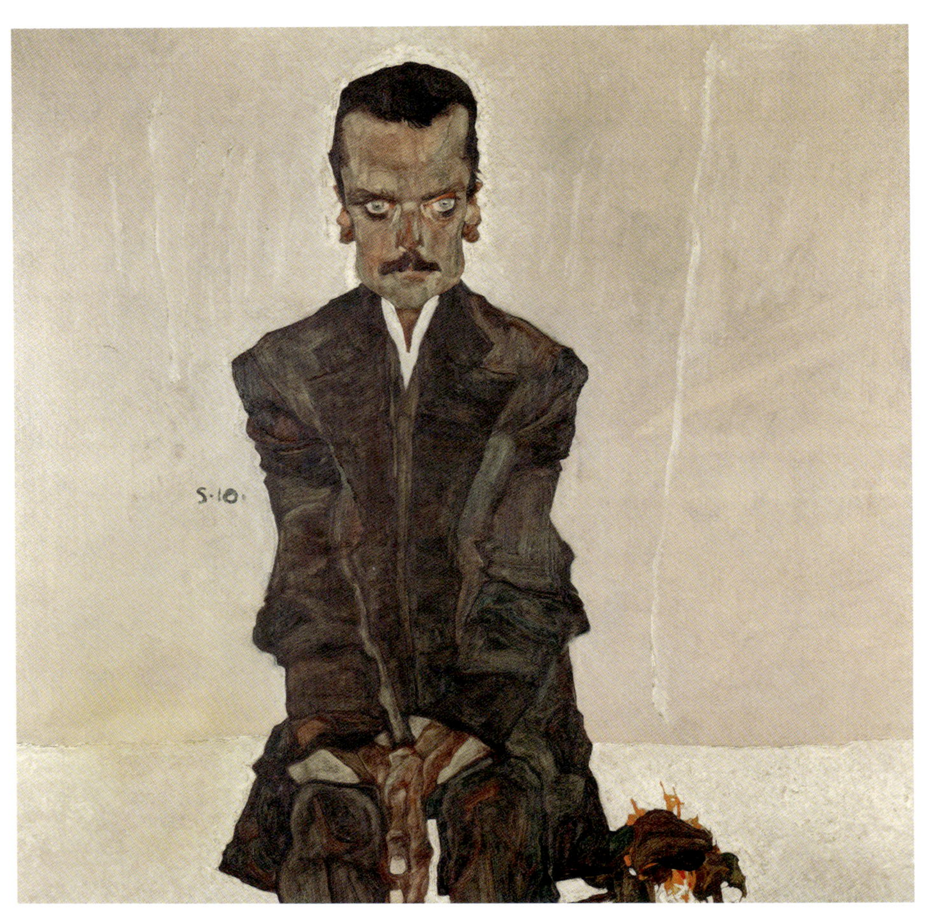

Egon Schiele

Eduard Kosmack
1910

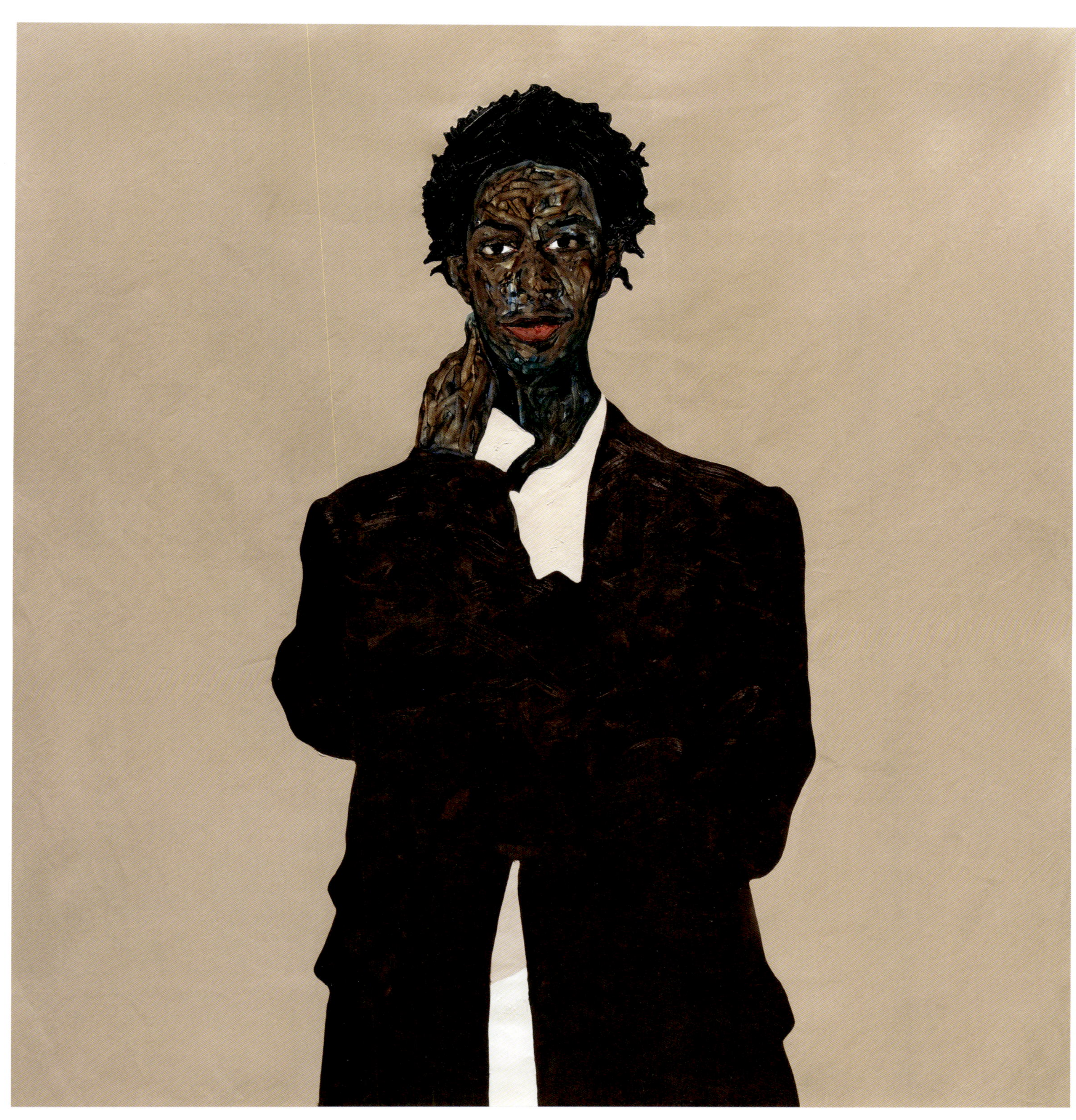

Jean-Michel Basquiat IV
2020

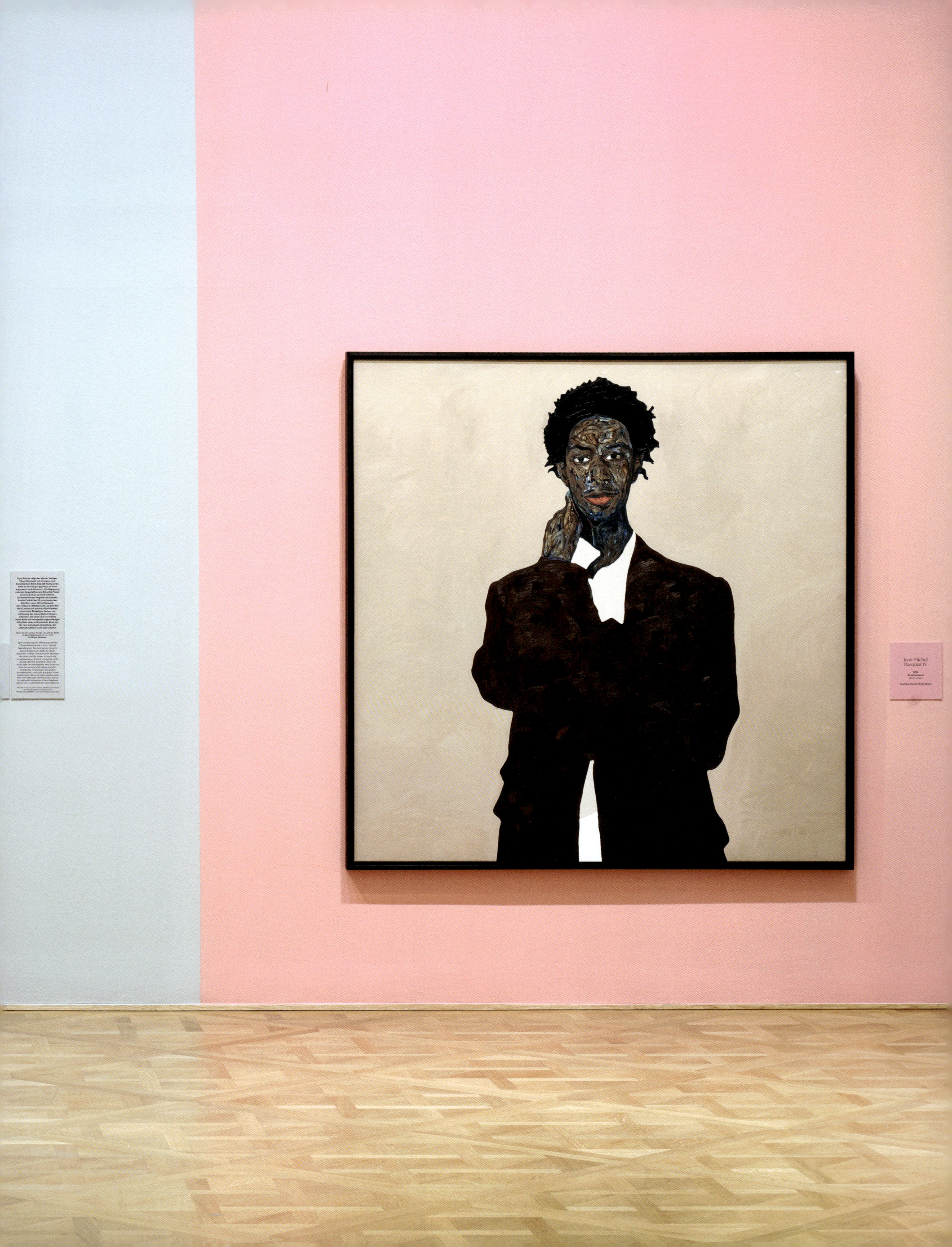

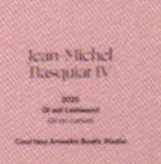
Jean-Michel
Basquiat IV
2020
Oil on Linwood
Courtesy Amoako Boafo Studio

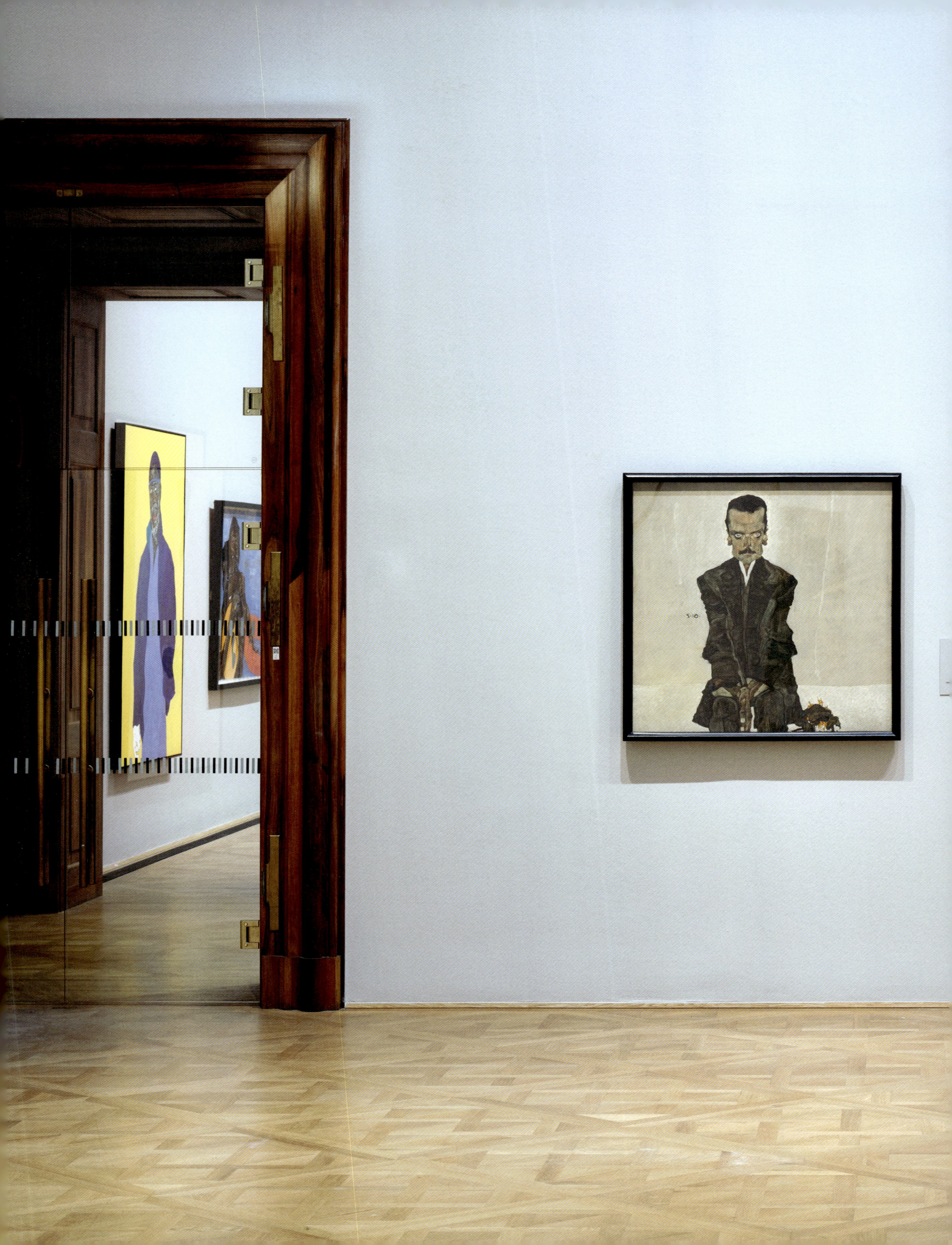

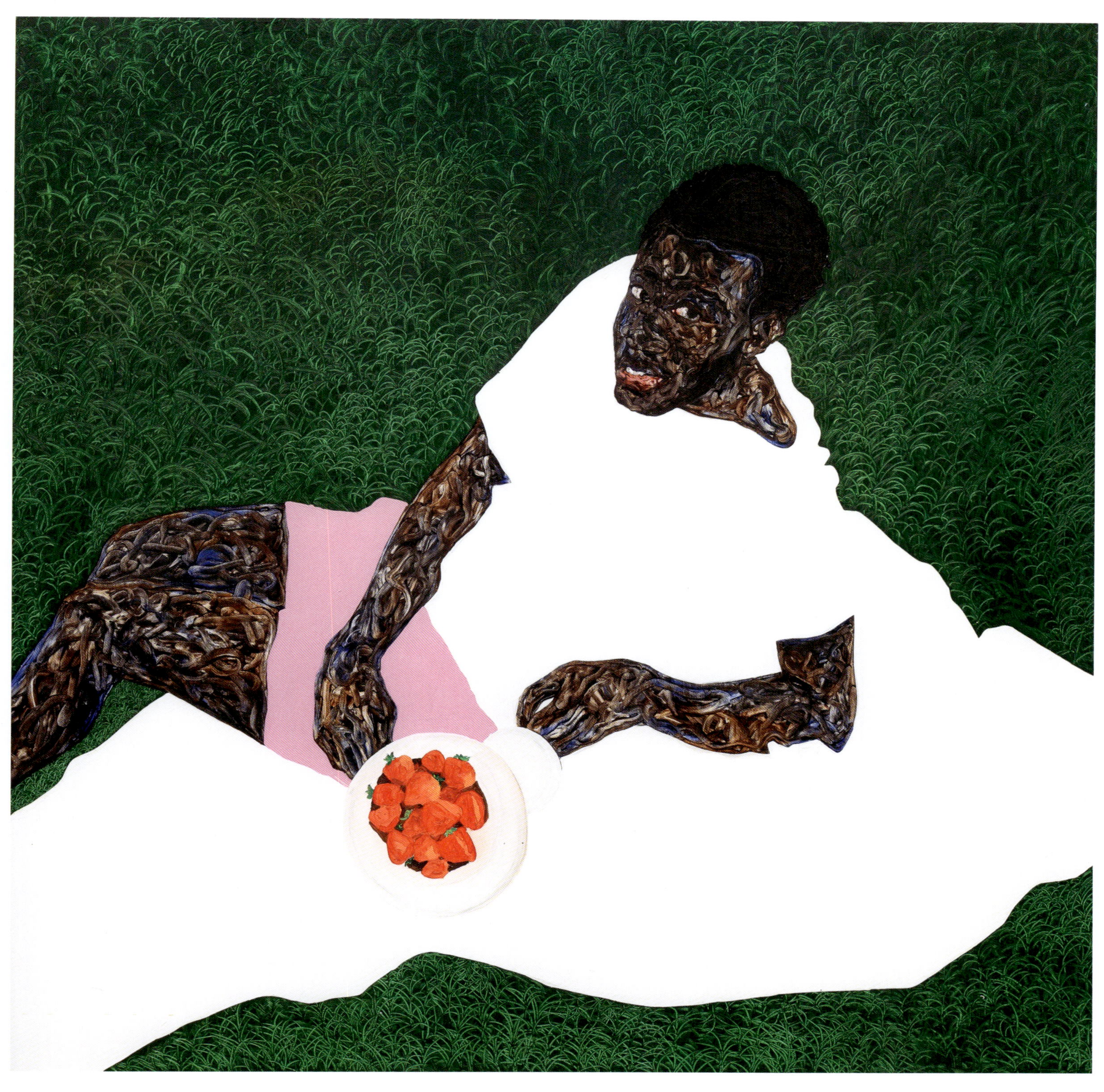

Strawberries and Pink Shorts
2022

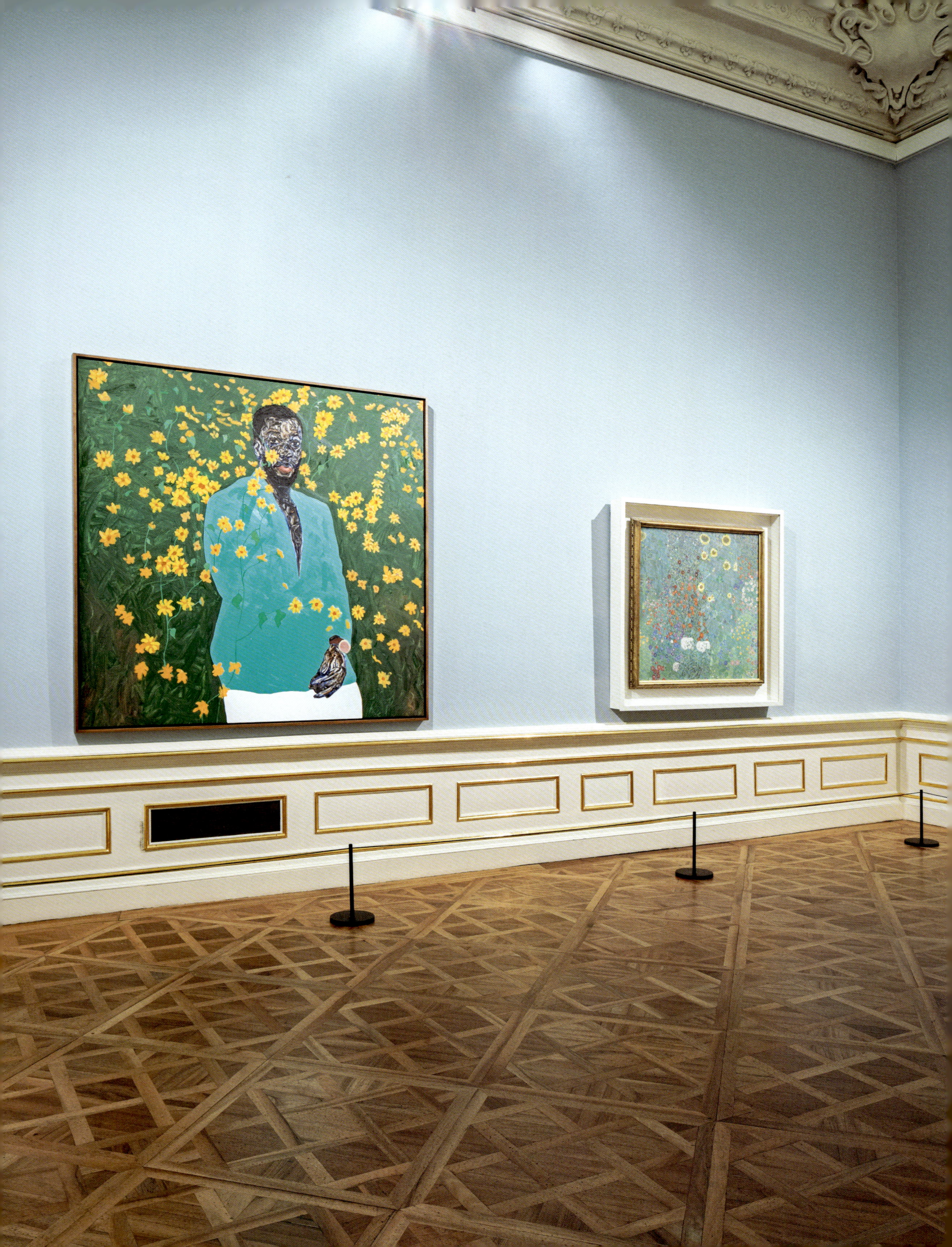

Sunflower Field, dating from 2022, has a special status within Amoako Boafo's oeuvre because, as the title clearly states, it incorporates the countryside as a key element in the staging and interpretation of the figure depicted. The painting shows a fashionably dressed man who, with his hands clasped, seems to be standing in the middle of a field of flowers. His naked chest is visible under his turquoise jacket. The casual expression of the man's face radiates openness and tenderness and is directed straight at the viewer. The eye-catching sunflowers of the title are painted in bright yellow and are scattered across the face and jacket of the person portrayed, creating the impression that are pulling the figure into the background.

Unlike Boafo's other works, which often feature an abstract, monochromatic background that clearly places the focus on the human figure, the person portrayed in *Sunflower Field* almost melds with the gestural brushstrokes of the field of flowers that fills the entire canvas. Alongside the highly expressive gestures and staging of his figures in space, during his years studying at the Vienna Academy of Fine Arts Vienna Boafo was also interested in the landscape painting of Viennese Modernism. This is highlighted by the juxtaposition of *Sunflower Field* with the landscapes of Austrian painter Gustav Klimt in the Upper Belvedere. The consciously flat manner in which the countryside is presented is striking, and there are no indications of perspective or a horizon. The setting in nature serves Boafo as a stage on which to present a contemporary notion of masculinity that has a modern echo due to the playfulness of the clothing and the floral themes.

Sunflower Field is in many respects a prime example of Boafo's painting that embraces Blackness in all manner of ways. With his emphatically fashionable clothing, the figure represented does not reflect a real person, but rather the idea of a specific Black self-confidence that is expressed in the choice of clothing and the form of self-stylization.[1] SH

1 Carol Tulloch, "Style—Fashion—Dress: From Black to Post-Black," *Fashion Theory*, yr. 14, no. 3 (2010), p. 276. See Mahret Ifeoma Kupka's essay in this catalogue, pp. 17–21.

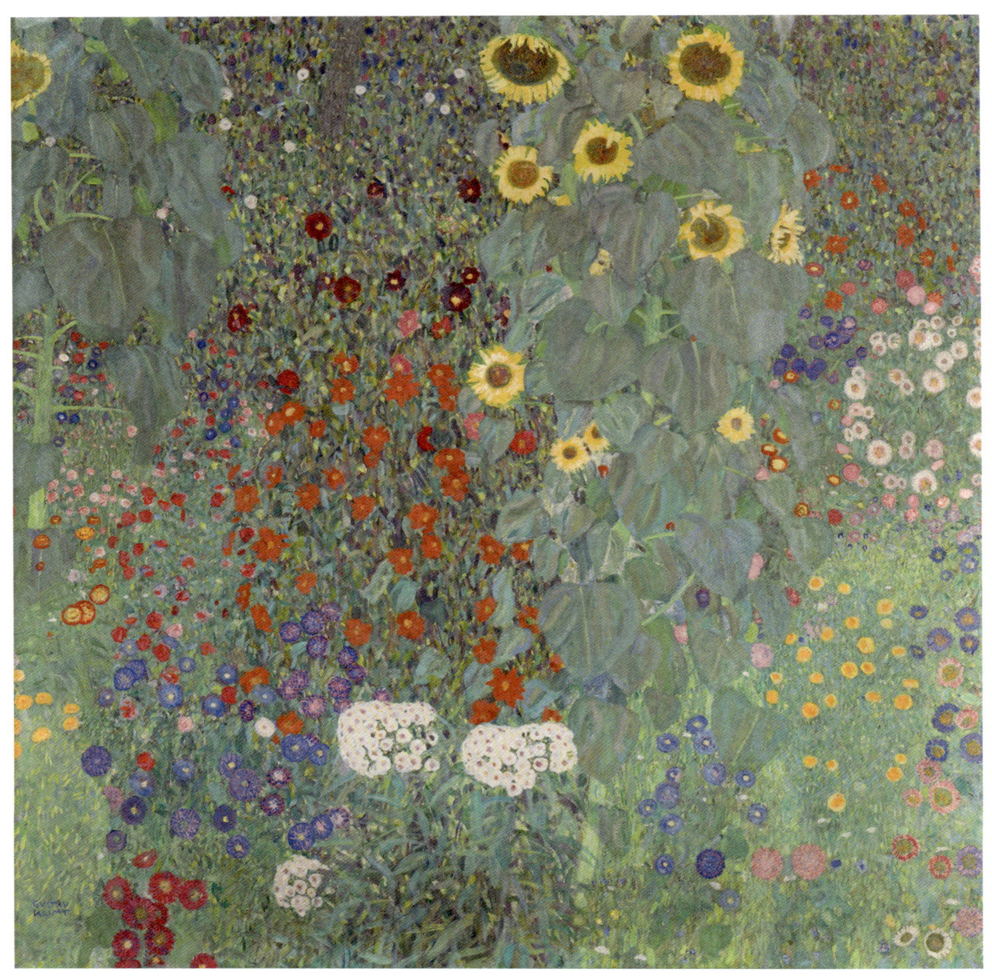

Gustav Klimt

Cottage Garden with Sunflowers
1906

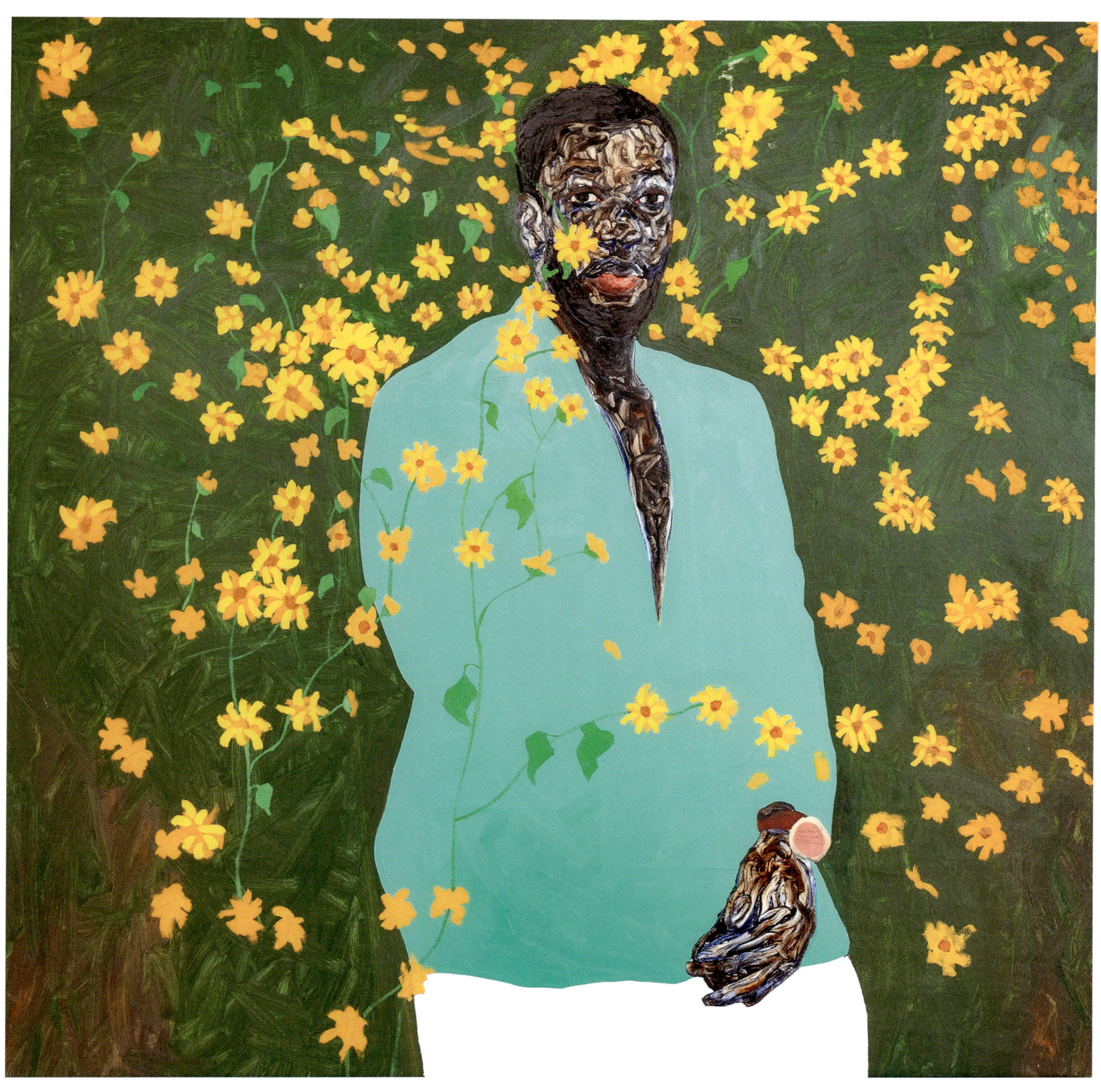

Sunflower Field

2022

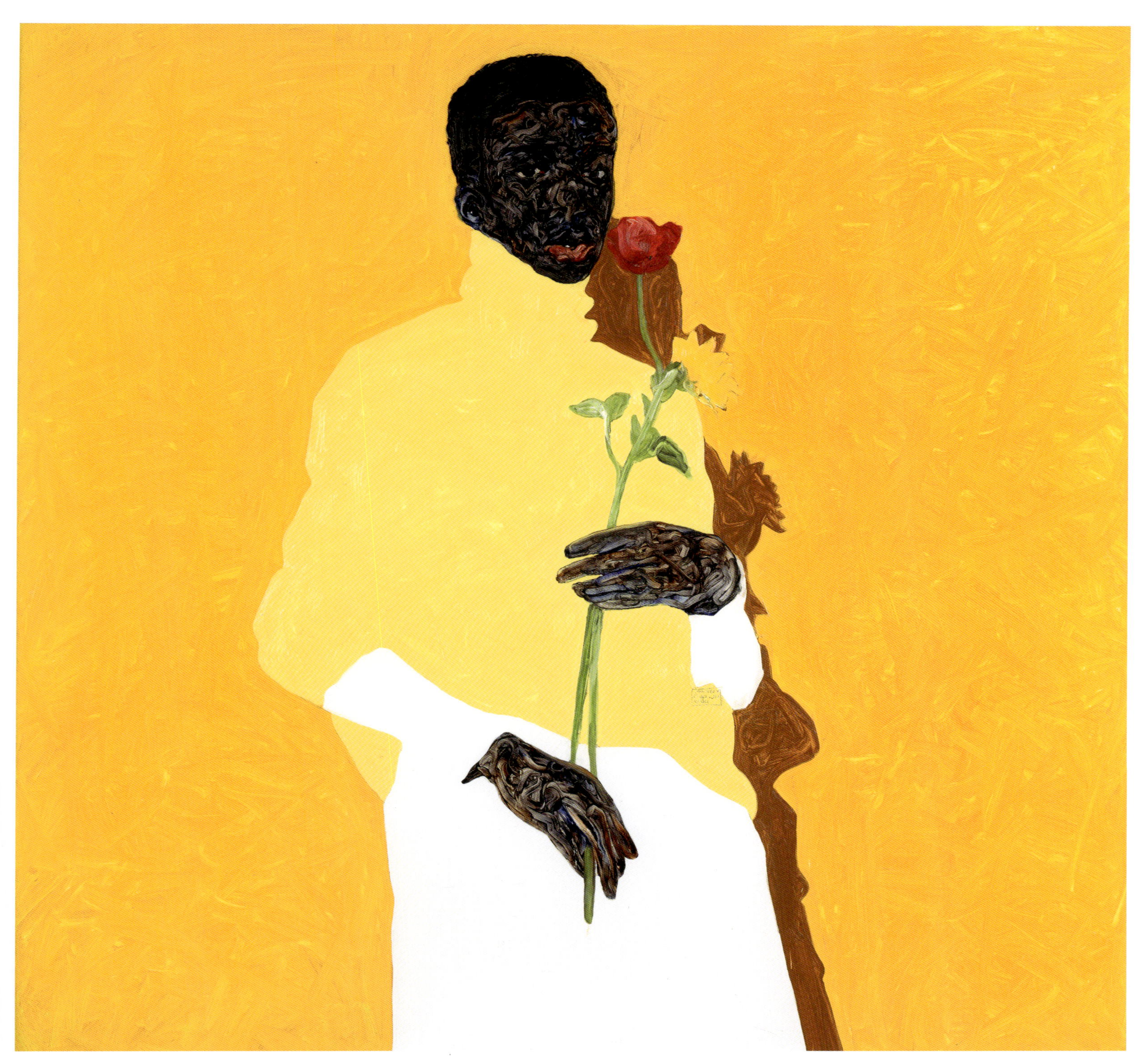

Yellow Turtleneck

2021

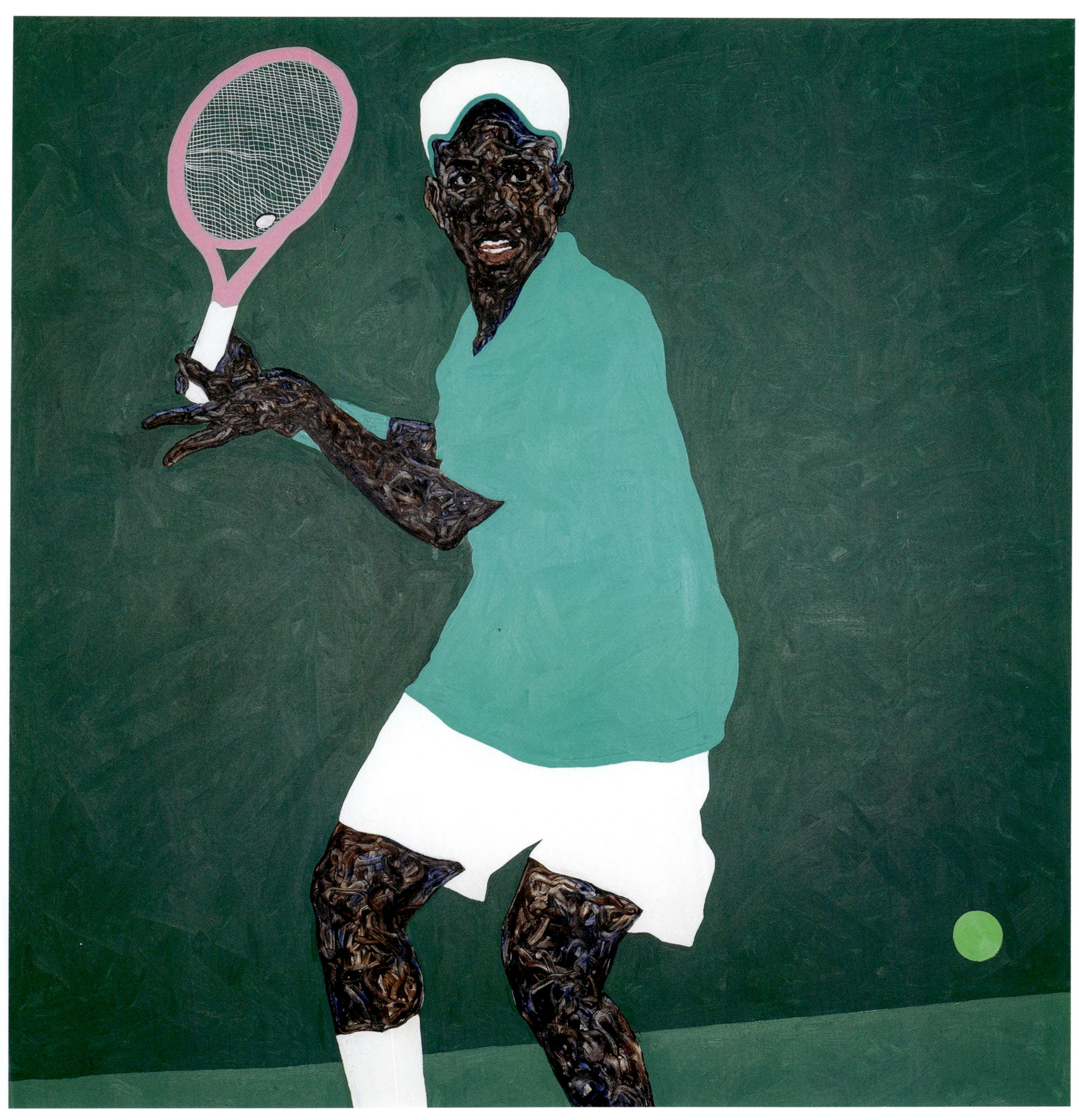

Mr. Palm—Green Wristband
2022

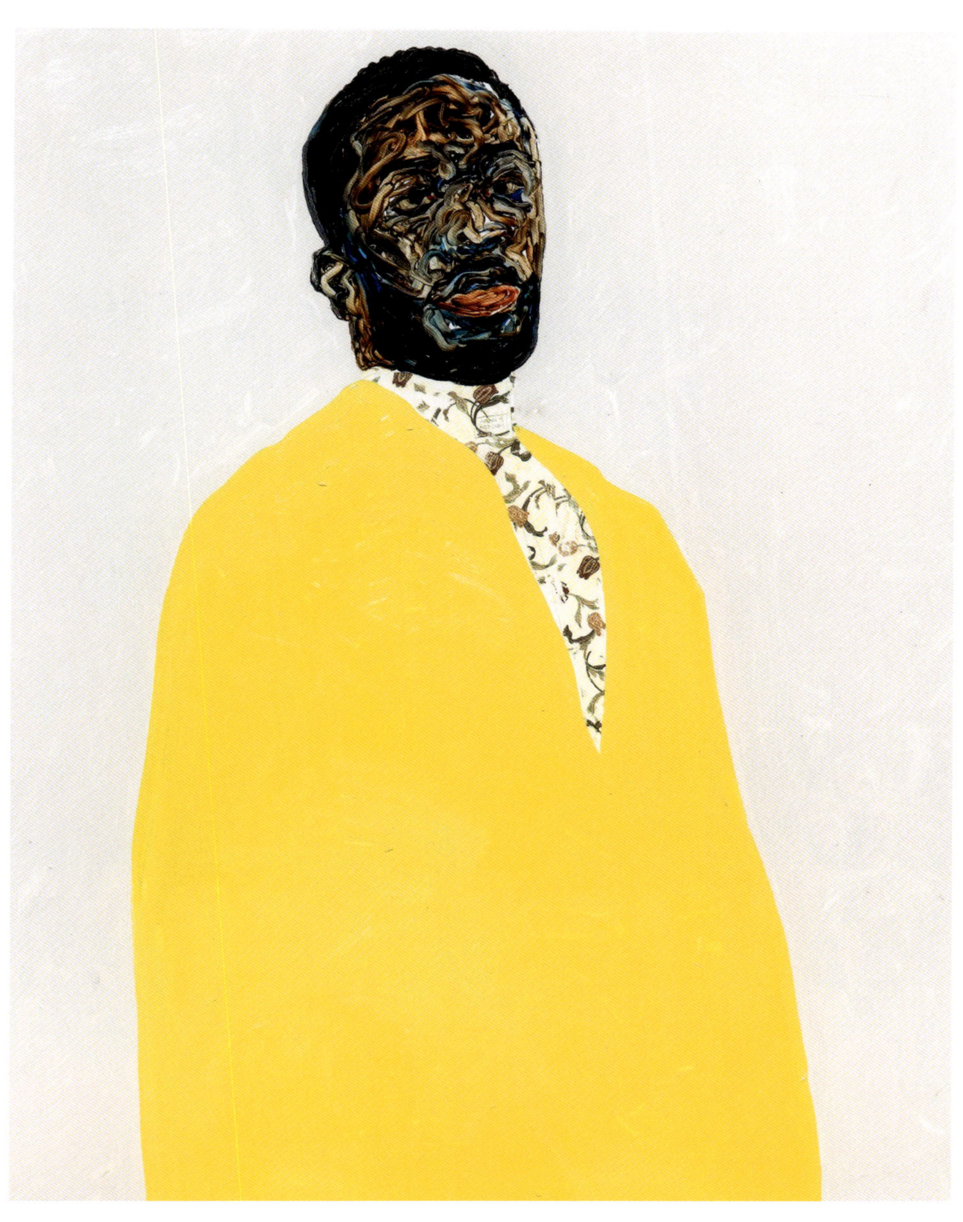

Yellow Jacket
2020

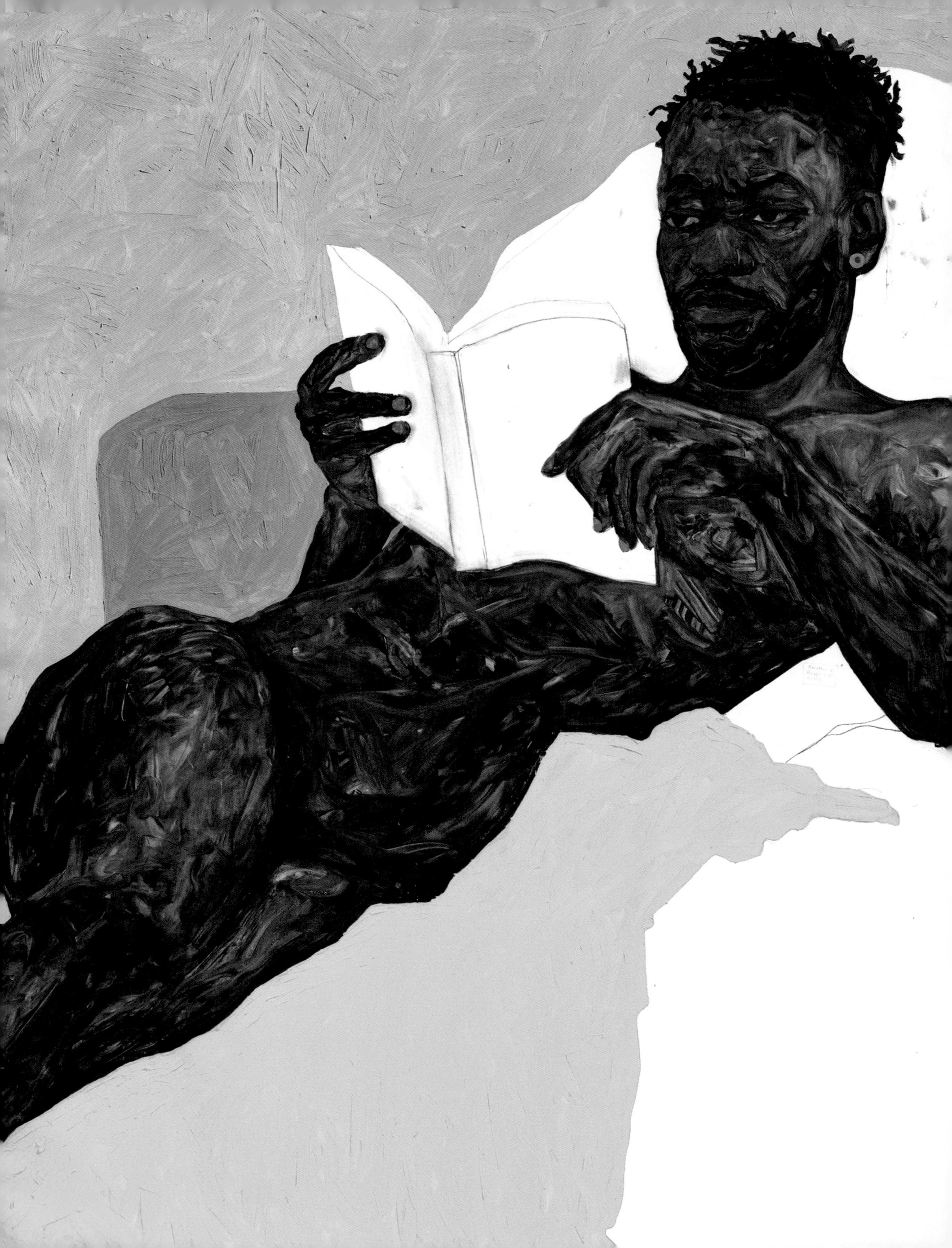

Self-Portraits

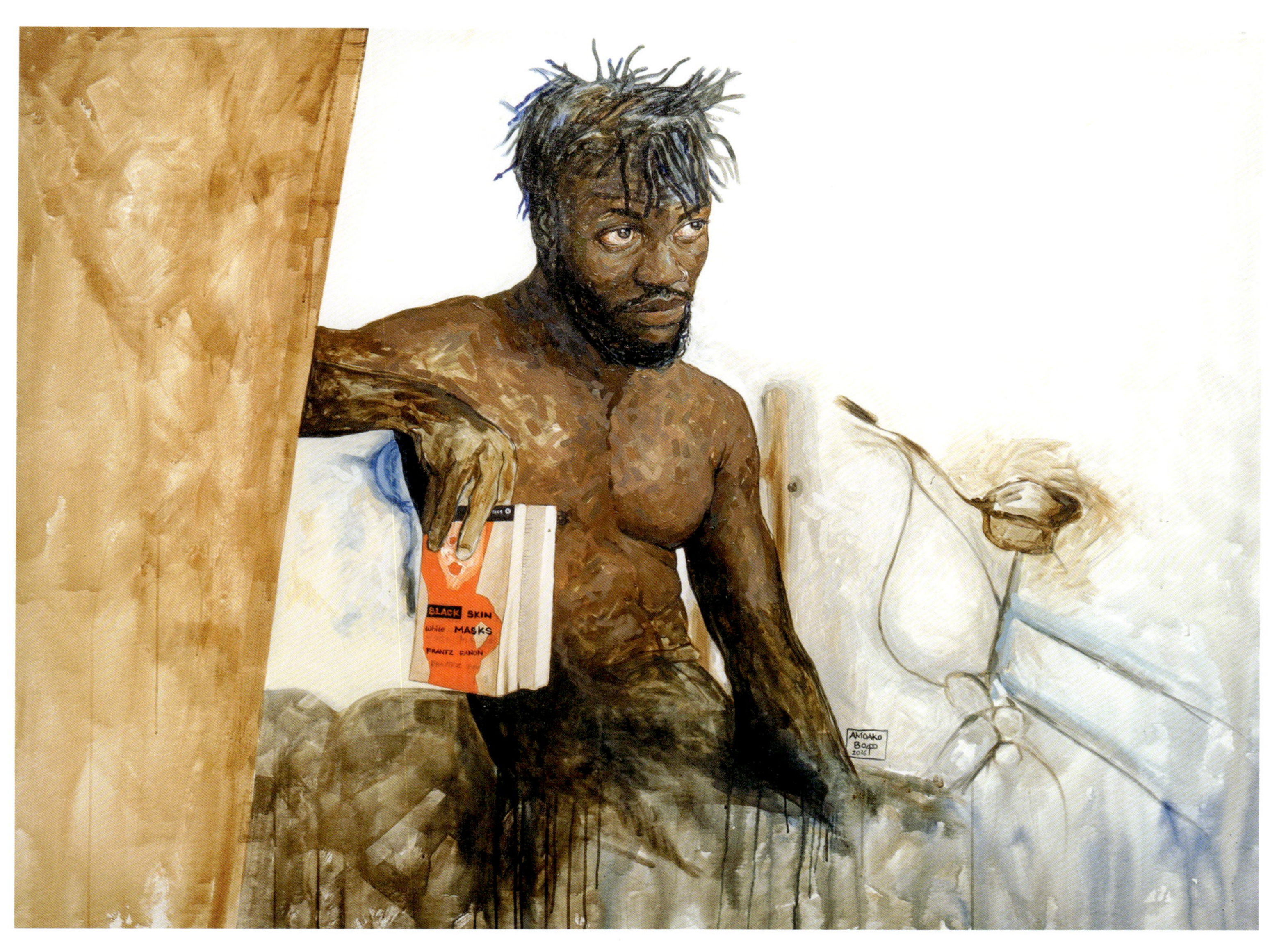

Black Skin, White Mask
2016

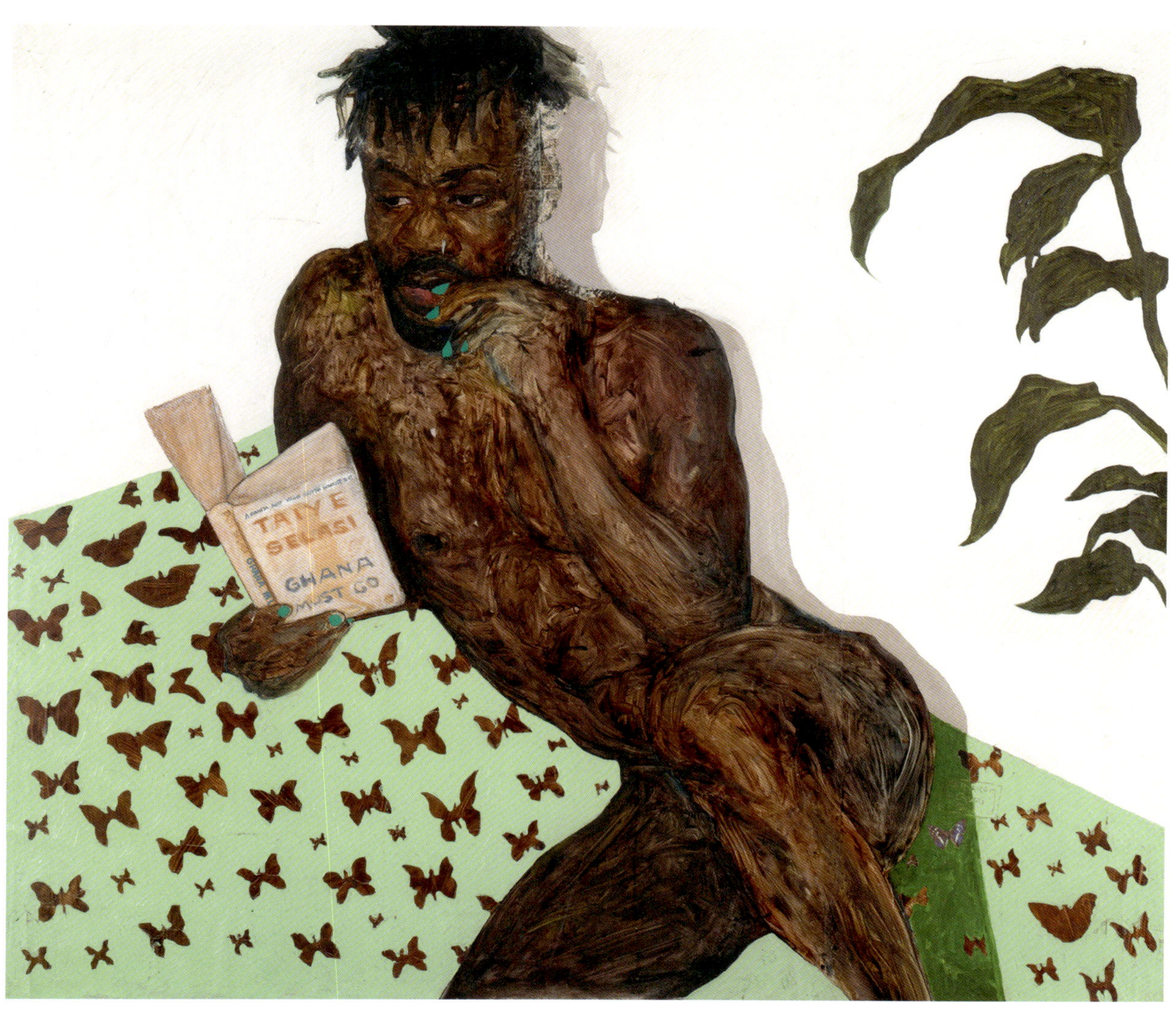

Ghana Must Go
2017

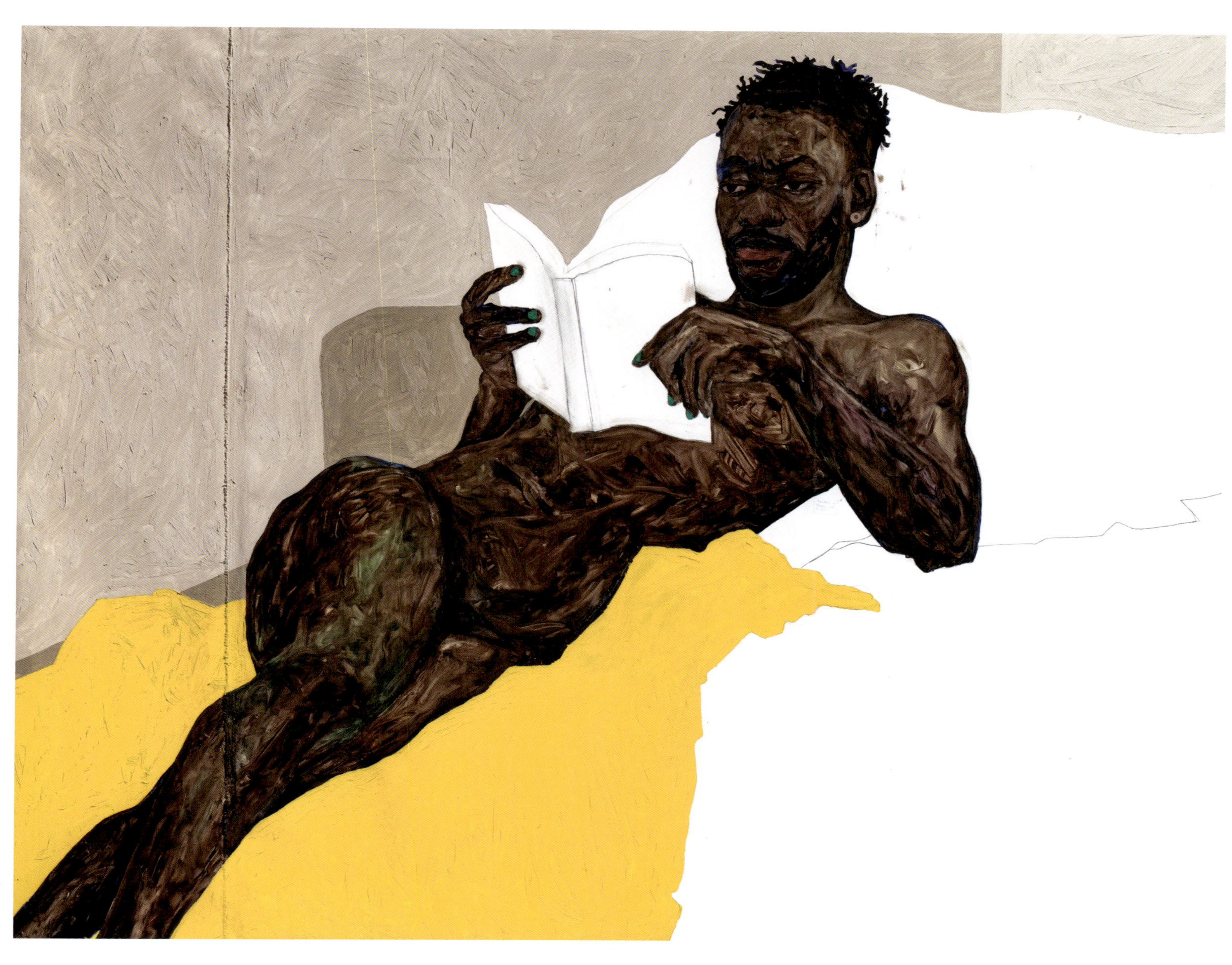

Yellow Blanket
2018

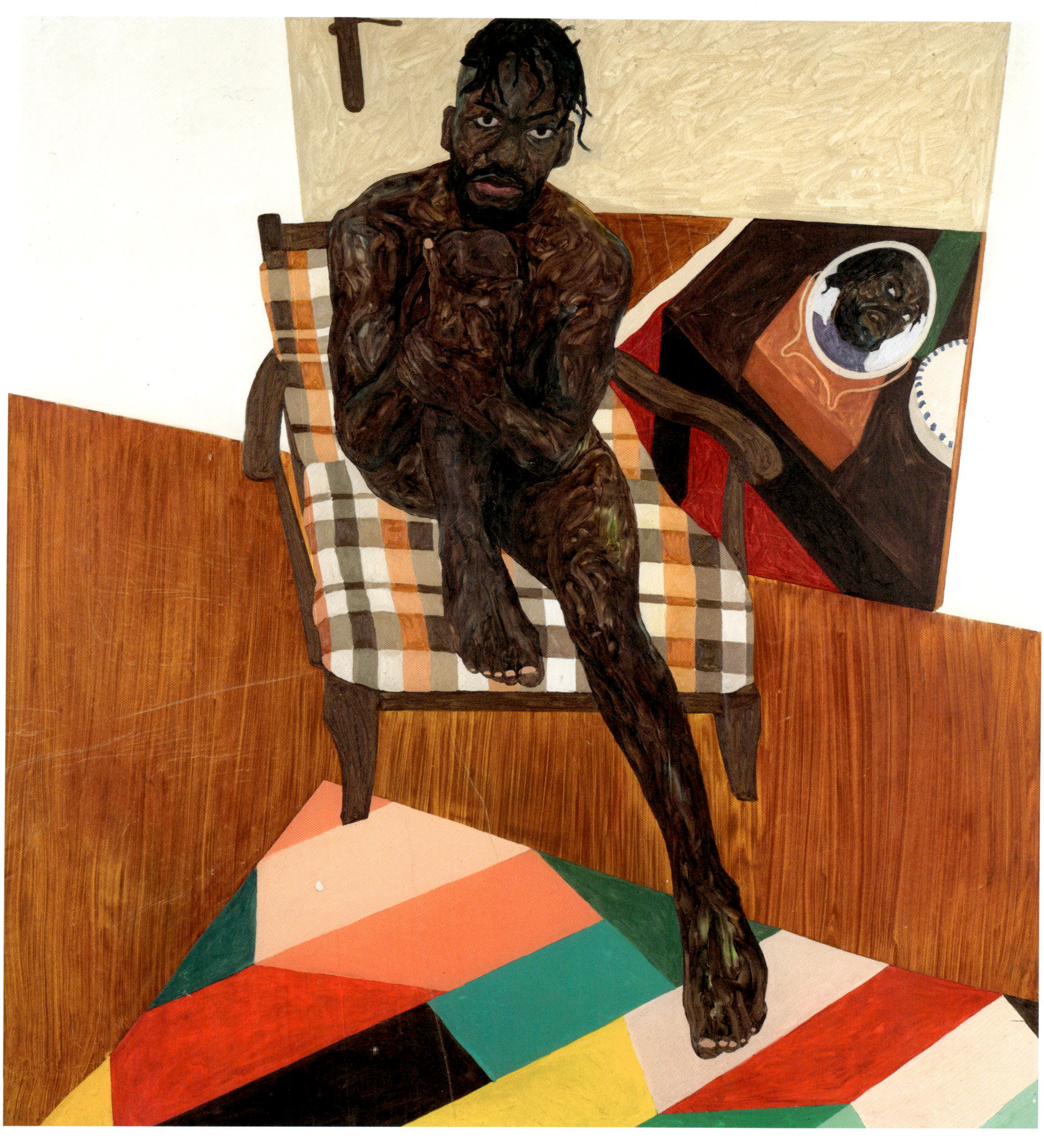

Angry Boy
2018

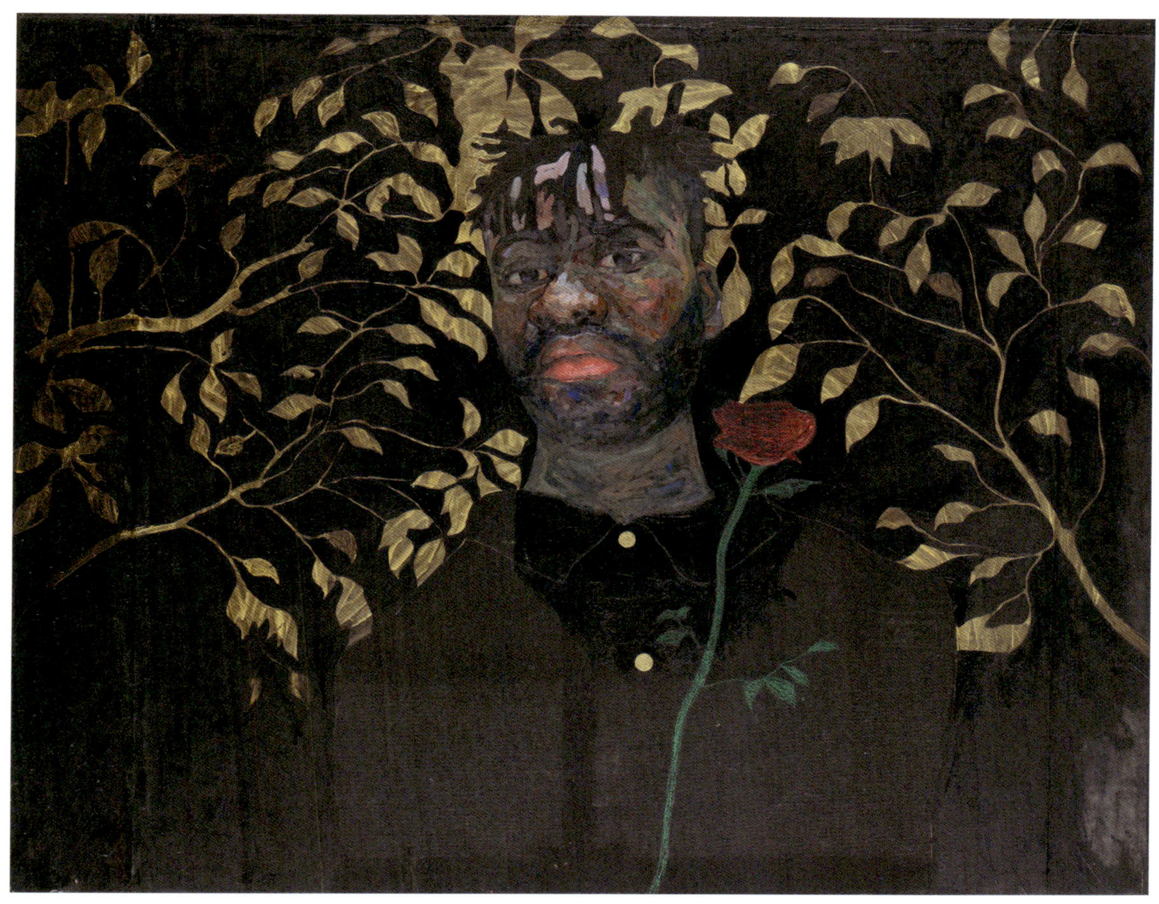

Gold Leaves
2017

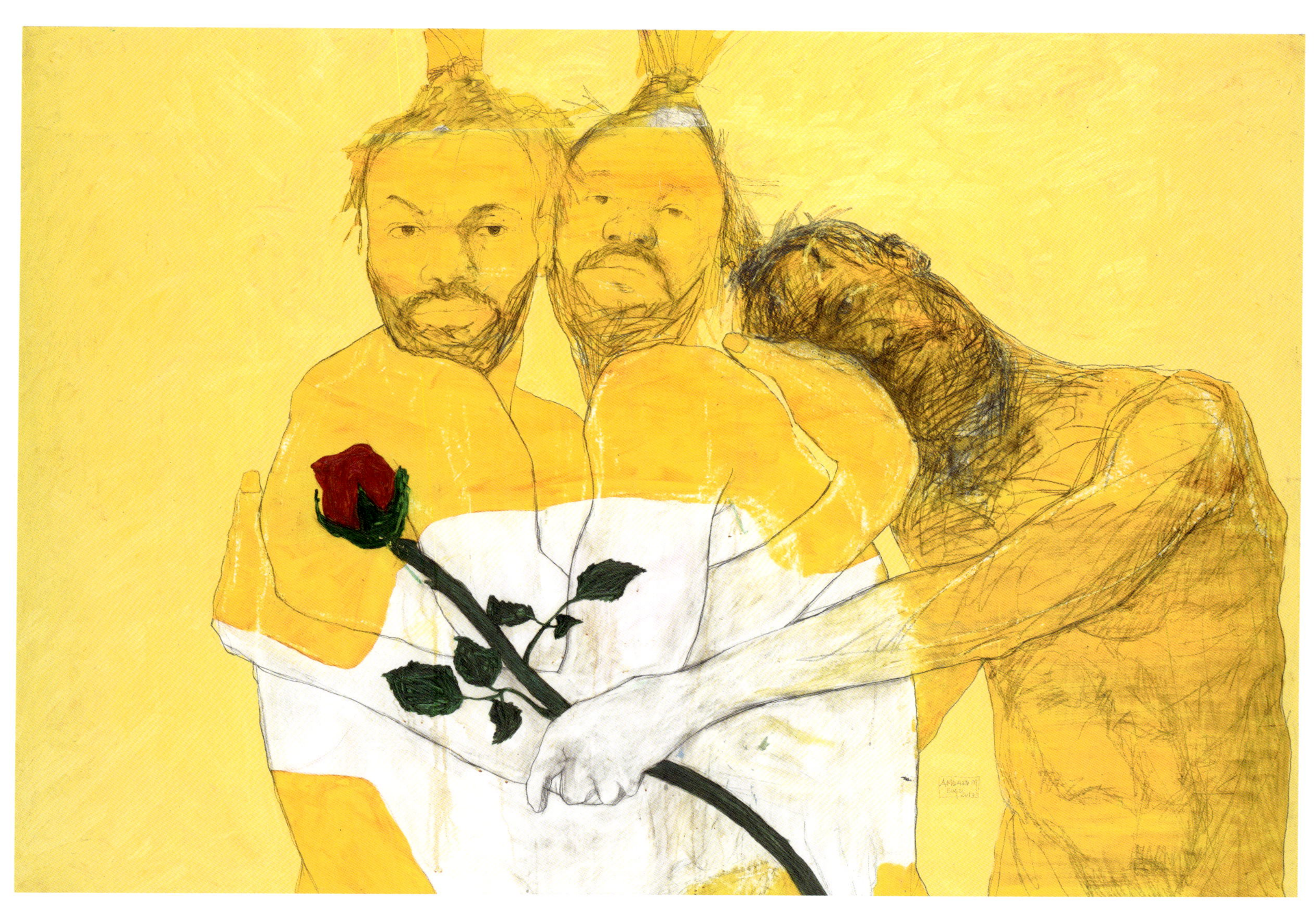

Me, Me, and Me
2017

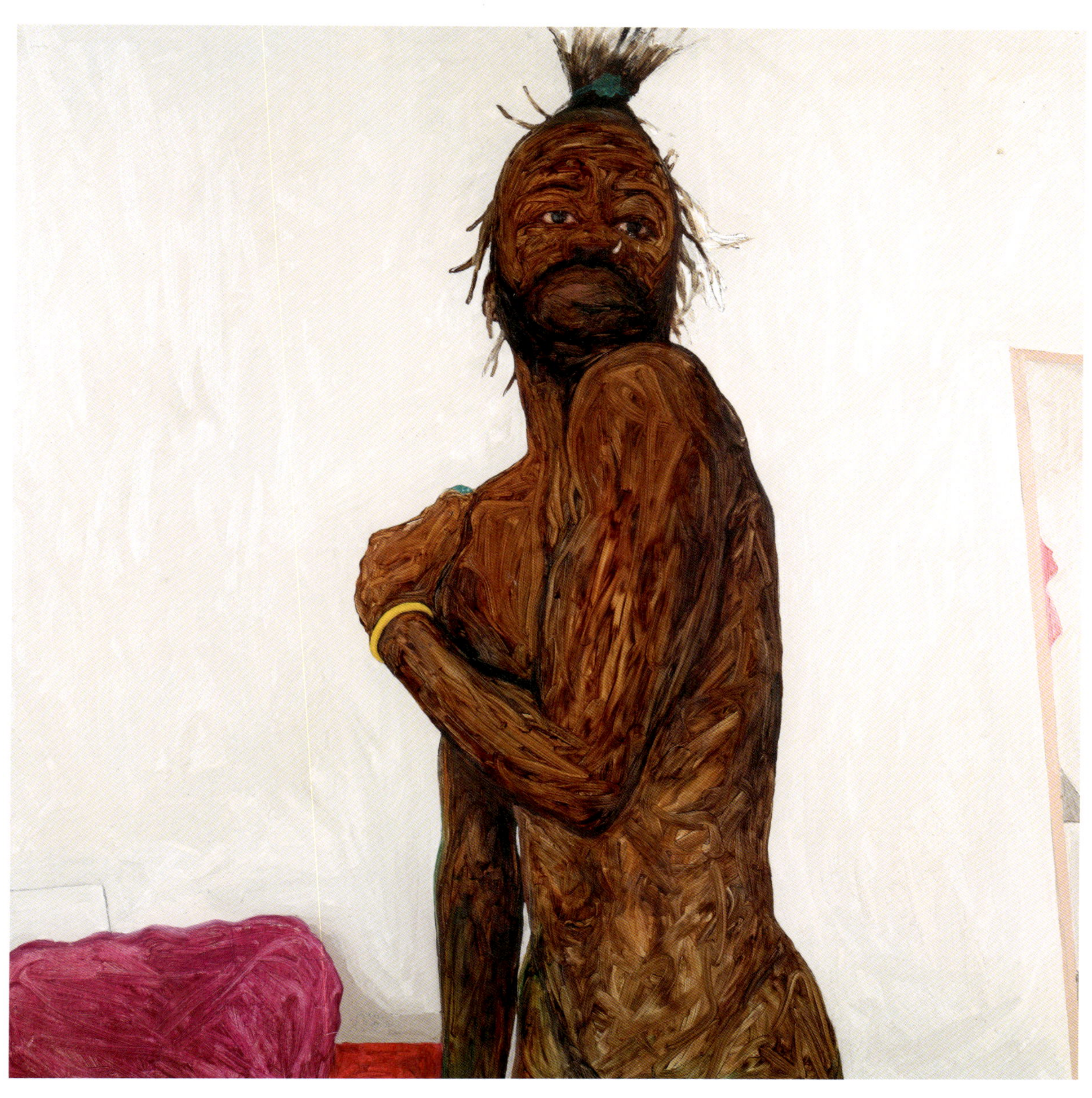

Blue Band
2017

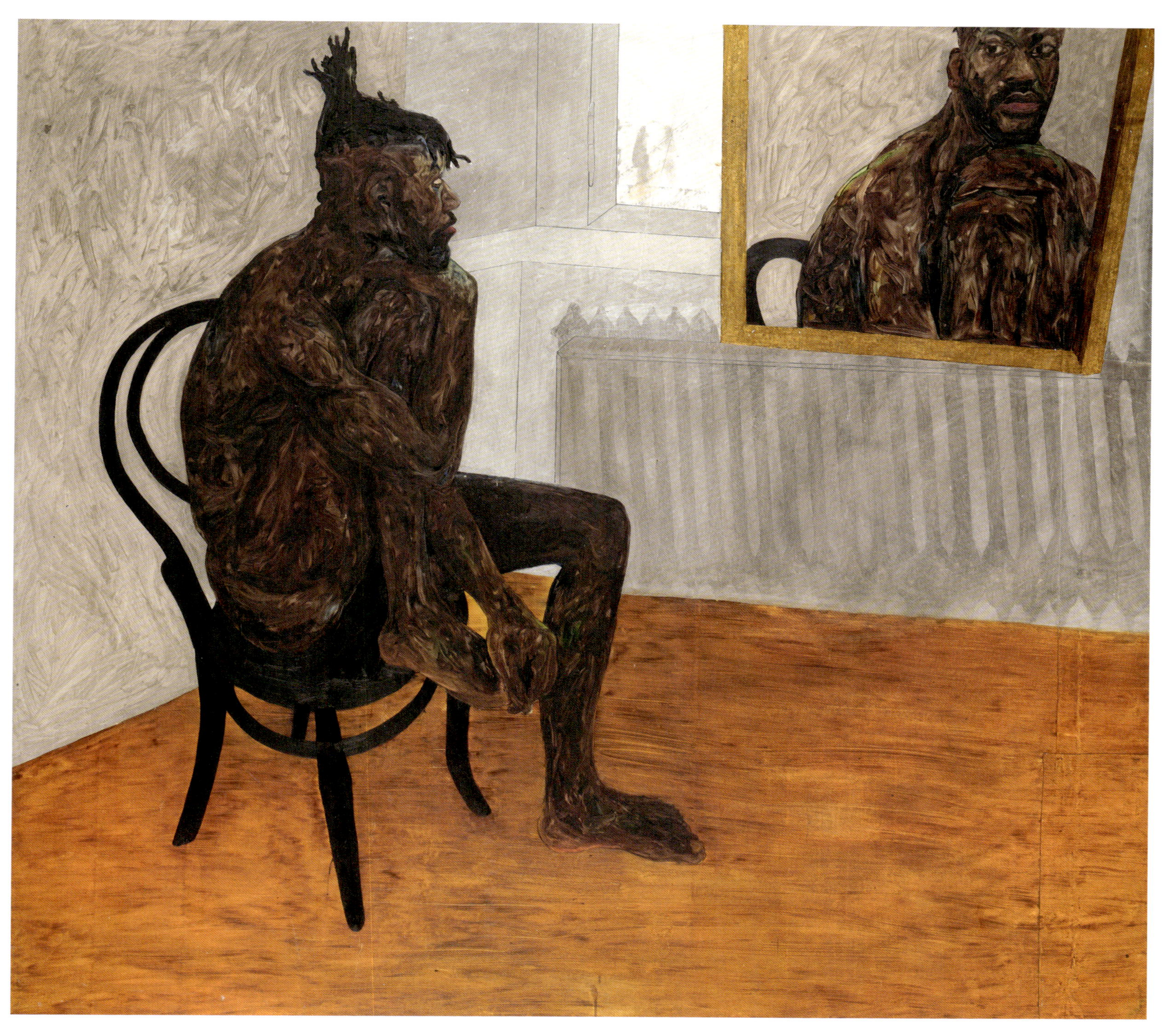

Reflection II
2018

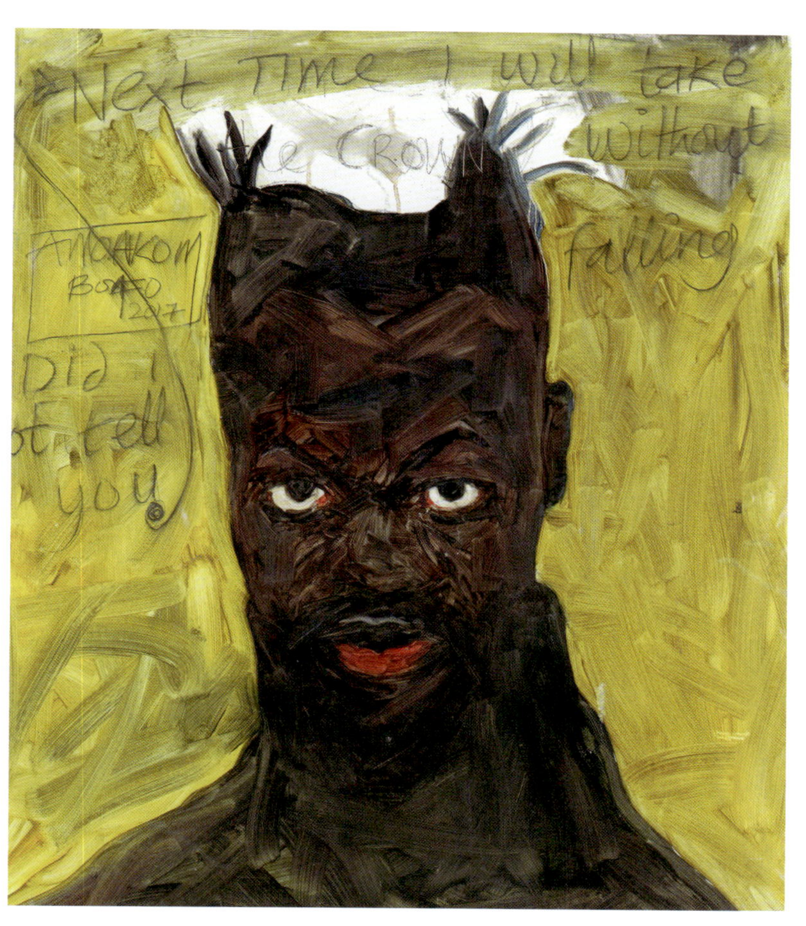

Self Portrait—Taking The Crown II
2017

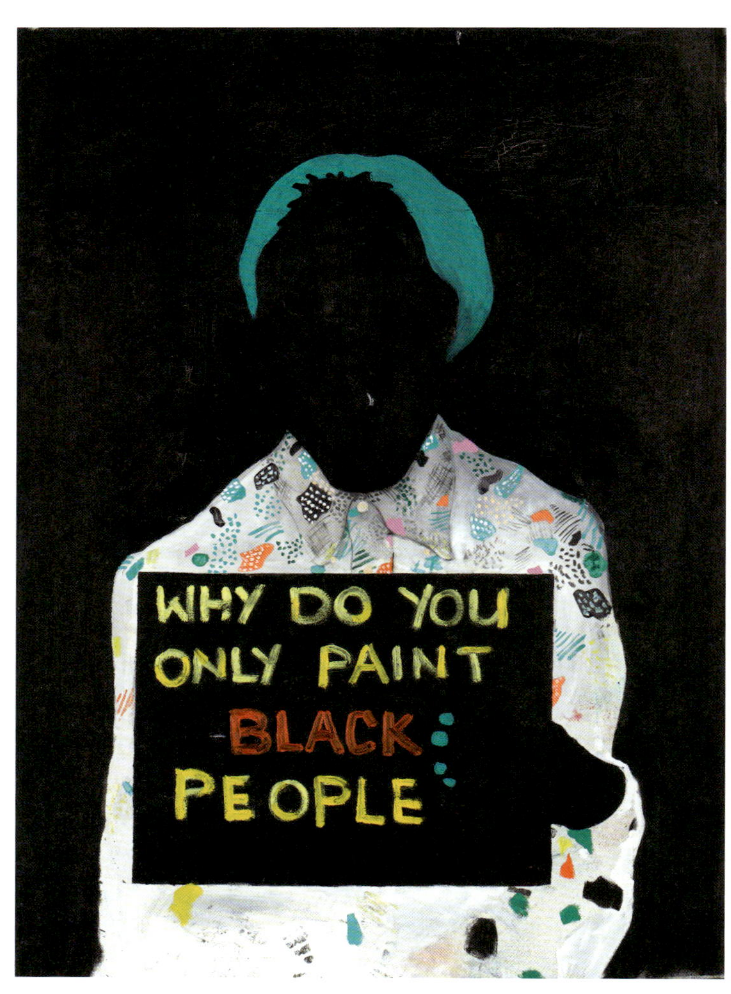

Why Do You Only Paint Black People
2017